D1373369

Sunday School Promo Pages

Reproducible Advice, Answers and Articles on How to Build a Strong and Healthy Sunday School at Your Church

By WES & SHERYL HAYSTEAD

Gospel Light

How to make clean copies from this book

You may make copies of portions of this book if:

- you (or someone in your organization) are the original purchaser.
- you are using the copies you make for a noncommercial purpose (such as teaching or promoting a ministry) within your church or organization.
- you follow the instructions provided in this book.

However, it is illegal for you to make copies if:

- you are using the material to promote, advertise or sell a product or service other than for ministry fund-raising.
- you are using the material in or on a product for sale.
- you or your organization are **not** the original purchaser of this book.

By following these guidelines you help us keep our products affordable. Thank you.

Gospel Light

Gospel Light

Contents for this manual can sure come in handy

Indexed list makes each item easy to find

CHAPTER ONE

Parable of the Perplexed Promoter
OR How to Use This Manual

She was bright.

She was eager.

She was dedicated.

She was the newly appointed leader of children's ministries in her church.

And she was so, so naive.

The room looked great.

The refreshments looked appetizing.

The guest speaker looked prepared.

And the chairs looked so, so empty.

"I just can't understand where everyone is!" she exclaimed after making yet another nervous stroll to the window to look at the nearly empty parking lot. "We should have more than 60 people here tonight," she announced as she once again compared the time on her watch with that showing on the wall clock.

"It certainly is difficult to get people to come out on a week night," the guest speaker commented in an effort to ease the evident disappointment.

"But I put it in the bulletin for two Sundays!" the children's director wailed.

As we said, she was naive. Somehow, she really thought that two bulletin notices would do the trick, causing over threescore people to appear at this meeting.

We also said she was eager. Eager to learn and eager to become effective in children's ministry. Thus, she asked the right question as she and the guest speaker and the half dozen faithful regulars began tackling the refreshment table: "What did I do wrong?"

Carefully commenting while chewing a gooey fudge brownie, the guest speaker suggested: "I haven't seen the bulletin, but there was probably nothing wrong with what you wrote. The problem is probably more what you didn't do right."

"What should I have done?" she asked, sitting down and taking out a notebook and pencil.

The refreshment table was stocked for an army and everyone in that small group had planned to be at the church for another 90 minutes or so. Thus, the evening proceeded into a wide-ranging discussion and a wide-reaching buffet. The buffet focused on chocolate. The discussion targeted actions needed to effectively promote the ministry of the Sunday School.

Between bites, the children's director and her faithful staff peppered the guest with a steady stream of questions:

✦ "How DO you get teachers or parents to come to a meeting?"

✦ "How do you GET enough teachers to begin with?"

✦ "How do YOU get the church to realize the value of Sunday School and children's ministry?"

✦ "HOW do you get parents to bring their children regularly instead of just when it's convenient?"

✦ "How do you get KIDS excited about Sunday School?"

✦ "But I'm an EDUCATOR! I've been called to MINISTER! You sound like I'm supposed to become a PROMOTER!?" (Granted, this was not really a question, but her voice did go up at the end and her face looked very puzzled. So, more about this one later.)

Anyhow, you get the idea.

What IS This Manual?

As you read through this manual, you'll get the answers that were shared that night, plus a great deal more that weren't thought of in spite of all that dessert. In addition, you'll find a host of ideas and practical resources you can use to implement all those good answers. (Unfortunately, you have to provide your own chocolate.)

In other words, **this manual is a collection of ready-to-use resources and plans to encourage Sunday School attendance and create enthusiasm about the ministry of the Sunday**

School. The book is filled with ideas that have been successfully used in both large and small churches. These ideas are based on the premise that anyone who wants to have an effective Sunday School or other ministry with children must give some major attention to the matter of promotion, publicity, public relations—salesmanship. Program goals, benefits and plans must be communicated effectively—to children, parents, teachers, church leaders, the congregation, the community!

Proper PROMOTION PRODUCES Plenty of PEOPLE in Your Program

The target below shows how this book is organized.

Each succeeding chapter focuses on one target audience with whom you must communicate in order for your Sunday School to flourish. We start with the children themselves, the ones for whom the ministry is intended. Then, gradually, our aim expands to include all those who need to learn the values of the Sunday School, to discover their part in the exciting work of reaching and teaching children.

Each chapter has a brief introduction followed by a collection of ideas and guidelines. The chapters conclude with a variety of reproducible art and headlines for your use in implementing the ideas in that chapter. Ideas which have reproducible art in that chapter are marked with this symbol.

Tips for Using the Art

✦ Add text providing details which fit your church programs.

✦ Reduce or enlarge the size of the art to fit the format in which the art will be used.

✦ Reproduce your promotion material on brightly colored, sturdy paper to catch attention and encourage people to post the flier, brochure, handout, etc.

✦ Add color (e.g., use markers or glitter pens) to highlight a few key headlines or a segment of the art. (It's worth the time this takes!)

✦ Add stickers for decoration and variety.

NOTE: Pages 213-217 in chapter 8 include a variety of art depicting children and families. This art can easily be used along with the ideas in any of the other chapters. You will find that much of the art provided throughout the book can also be used with ideas in other chapters.

Sunday School Focus

While this book is useful for the total children's ministry, you will notice that we focus on Sunday School, still by far the largest and most influential children's ministry in the land. You will also quickly notice that every idea provided to promote Sunday School easily applies to any other children's ministry in your church (children's church, VBS, camp, club, choir, etc.).

A Disclaimer

These publicity and education ideas assume that a quality learning environment is available for children. If a program is poorly run, no amount of promotional effort will succeed in boosting attendance or improving morale. This does not mean that a program must be perfect before the ideas in this book will be effective. It does mean that your promotional efforts must go hand in hand with efforts to improve the program.

A Word About "Gimmicks"

Some of the ideas in this book border on being gimmicks. And a few probably cross well over that border into being full-blown gimmicks. Many people view gimmicks as less than honorable endeavors, considering them to be superficial at best, and manipulative at worst.

Before you evaluate the suitability of any "gimmicky" ideas, remember that a quality ministry cannot be built on gimmicks. (See "Disclaimer" above.) Gimmicks are useful devices when used within a balanced program. Consider them for the following purposes:

✦ To capture attention and interest of children and adults who have developed the ability to "tune out" your more traditional approaches. Often a familiar truth becomes meaningful when looked at in a fresh way.

✦ To help people relax and enjoy themselves. A touch of humor is very helpful in enabling people to lower their defenses and be themselves.

✦ To build bridges between spiritual matters and everyday life. Sometimes a gimmick is "just the ticket" to help a child or parent see a teacher or leader as a "normal" person with whom they can relate.

Just remember, gimmicks are rarely a panacea, but they can be an effective "shot-in-the-arm."

Planning Your Promotion Efforts

To get the most mileage from the ideas and resources in this manual, sit down with your leadership team and look ahead to the coming months.

✦ Identify the programs, goals and events you want to promote.

✦ Determine the "target" audiences for your promotion efforts.

✦ Schedule your promotional activities to provide adequate "lead time" before each event.

The sample Promotional Calendar on page 9 illustrates how leaders in one church planned their promotional activities. (All activities mentioned are suggested in later chapters.) It's followed by a reproducible blank Promotional Calendar for you to use in scheduling events in your own church.

Promotional Calendar

SEPTEMBER Special Invitations to Kids Letters to Parents Newsletter Announcements Teachers' Meeting	**OCTOBER** Open House Teacher Treat Day Congregation Prayer Reminders	**NOVEMBER** Donut Day Map—kids mark homes
DECEMBER Letter to Families about special events	**JANUARY** Video Day Teachers' Meeting New Year's Handout to Church Neighborhood	**FEBRUARY** Poster Contest Meet the Pastor Day
MARCH Friendship Day Bible Learning Activity sharing in Worship service Display Posters Interview S.S. teacher in Worship	**APRIL** Send Recruiting Letters and Follow Up Bulletin and Newsletter Inserts Skit in Worship Easter Postcards	**MAY** Picture Day
JUNE VBS Teacher Thank-you Cards	**JULY** Class Parties VBS Follow-up	**AUGUST** Game Day

Promotional Calendar

SEPTEMBER	OCTOBER	NOVEMBER
DECEMBER	JANUARY	FEBRUARY
MARCH	APRIL	MAY
JUNE	JULY	AUGUST

CHAPTER TWO

Concentrate on Children

COMMUNITY
CONGREGATION
CHURCH LEADERS
NEW TEACHERS
TEACHERS
PARENTS
CHILDREN

"My husband and I both work full time," a mom told me. "So Tucker's in day care until 6:00 each evening. On weekends, I just don't have the heart to make him go to Sunday School if he doesn't want to go."

"Frankly, I wanted to sleep in and read the paper this morning," a dad grumbled. "But Amber was up and dressed and anxious to go. I didn't have the heart to tell her we weren't coming to church."

The most important people to convince that Sunday School is a great place for kids—are the kids. Not to say that parents aren't important (see chapter 3). It's just a fact of life. Sooner or later, the child who is not attracted to Sunday School simply will no longer be there. And the child who has learned that Sunday School is worthwhile and enjoyable, will be.

The attention-getting tools and ideas in this chapter are no substitute for a quality learning experience. As children get older they develop a keen suspicion about adults promising one thing but delivering something very different ("Try it, you'll like it." "Right."). All we can say is, the approaches suggested in this chapter have proven effective in building a positive attitude towards Sunday School among the ultimate consumers, including children who attend regularly, those who attend occasionally, and those who have never attended before. (These ideas appeal to both older and younger children. However, older

children may respond more positively if the activity is planned uniquely for them and does not involve younger children.)

These ideas might appeal to you for use at special times:
✦ kick-off in the fall;
✦ Vacation Bible School follow-up;
✦ outreach emphasis;
✦ special events or seasonal emphases.

You'll also find they work just as well as "shot-in-the-arm" ideas at any time throughout the year—whenever you feel enthusiasm and attendance are slacking off a little or when things are going great and you want to keep the momentum high.

Many of the ideas in this chapter are for use by teachers or departmental leaders. The "Teachers' Meetings" section on pages 106 and 107 in chapter 4 contains specific suggestions for encouraging and equipping teachers to use these ideas with their classes.

Theme Days

PP.19-23
Reproducible

Everybody knows about Mother's Day and Father's Day (that's the same as Mother's Day except you buy a cheaper present). These are among the special days on every-

body's calendar that tend to boost Sunday School attendance (it's hard to top Easter Sunday for drawing a crowd). And there are days that do just the opposite (Memorial Day and Labor Day are tough on churches in our town). Why not invent some special days—just for kids—that get them excited about coming to Sunday School? Who wouldn't want to be there on—
✦ Donut Day?
✦ Picture Day?
✦ Crazy Hat Day?
✦ Island Day?

Theme days capture the interest of children, while giving teachers a great excuse to contact kids with some good news. Theme days are terrific vehicles for inviting new children to visit and attracting absentees and dropouts to return. They even help make the irregular come more regularly—and the faithful few who never miss will come more enthusiastically, often with a friend in tow!

Theme days also allow kids and teachers to have a little fun together, which goes a long way towards building better teacher/child relationships. These theme days are designed just for fun, with no intention to tie into the lesson. Though there really is a connection—by starting with something of obvious appeal to the child, we capture attention and earn the child's willingness to listen when we have something else to say. Basically, theme days help "de-stufficize" the grown-ups in Sunday School, making us seem a little more human to the children we want to reach, and love, and teach.

Tips for Organizing and Publicizing

1. Plan two to four theme days a year.

2. Schedule a theme day about two months in advance.

3. Use or adapt the ideas provided to plan some theme-related activities on that day. These activities may replace one or more of the usual activities in the session. However, many of the theme day activities may be done as children arrive or be incorporated into the regular lesson activities.

4. Start promoting the day, using the lettering and art we provide to make postcards, fliers, name tags, mini-posters, bulletins/newsletters, classroom signs, banners, buttons, etc.

Picture Day

Take a picture of the entire Sunday School, each class, each individual or family. Subjects may be posed in front of a backdrop (a bulletin board headed "A Very Special Class," "This Kid Is Terrific," "Jesus Loves...," etc.) or with a congenial "celebrity" (Pastor? Teacher? Teenager?). You may also take candid shots of classes in action. Or, why not use a combination of these?

The pictures could be delivered to children later (a great excuse for a brief home visit), handed out the next Sunday (an incentive to come back next week), or posted on bulletin boards by the classroom door for parents to see. Consider mounting them in a Church Family Tree.

Crazy Hat Day

Make sure all the teachers and staff come appropriately attired. Offer a small prize to each child who comes wearing any type of headgear. And have bigger awards in each department or class, such as "Biggest Crazy Hat," "Smallest Crazy Hat," "Least Likely to Start a Fad," "Most Colorful," etc. Popular prizes include discount coupons to a favorite fast-food restaurant or Christian bookstore. (You can usually get these at no cost because of the free publicity you are giving the selected business.) Enlist various people in the congregation as judges (a great way to get some of your church leaders to pay a visit to children's classes). Do the judging right at the beginning of the session, then have a place designated where awkward or uncomfortable hats can be displayed until it's time to go home.

Donut Day

Besides the obvious snack to be served to everyone who attends, a donut motif can add some fun dimensions throughout the session:
✦ Prepare Bible verse puzzles on donut shaped poster board.
✦ Make a big donut cutout for a beanbag toss to be used with questions reviewing the Bible story (i.e., "Answer correctly and you get to hit the donut hole for 100 bonus points.").
✦ Letter words to songs on chart paper, drawing donuts in place of some of the key words. Ask children to suggest a variety of words that could be sung at those places.

Many other popular snacks could be used as the motif for a theme day, perhaps with a seasonal touch: **Ice Cream Day** in the summer; **Candy Apple Day** in the fall; **Popcorn Day** in winter; **Cookie Day** at any time.

Island Day or Western Day

These are great themes for classroom decorations, snacks, costumes and related games. For example, on Island Day you could provide plastic leis for children to wear, serve tropical punch as a snack, use a beach ball to play volleyball or build sand castles in your playground. On Western Day children will enjoy colorful bandanas to wear, western clothes in which to dress up for photos and eating homemade ice cream.

Video Day

Borrow enough VCR's and monitors so that every class or department can watch a Bible story or contemporary Christian video (available for rental or purchase from most Christian bookstores). Or, enlist parents with video cameras to capture some special classroom activities on video and play them back for the children. For example, record children singing, playing rhythm instruments, pantomiming or acting out the Bible story. Most Bible learning activities (art projects, games, etc.) gain new appeal and learning impact by being recorded on video and shown back.

Game Day

Change the format of the session by doing everything in game format. Play some games to help children and teachers get better acquainted, some just for fun, and others to help children learn or review Bible information. Your curriculum may provide Bible learning games or you may purchase game resources from your local Christian bookstore.

Sharing Day

This day is most popular and effective with children up through grades two or three. Each child brings a stuffed animal, book, or other favorite item to share with class. You may want to plan this day when the lesson topic relates (animals/creation; sharing with others).

Color Day

One of the easiest theme days to plan is Color Day. Each child is invited to wear one or two specified colors. Name tags, refreshments, etc., can be color coordinated.

Sports Day

Ask children to wear uniforms, T-shirts or clothing for sports they like to play or watch. Encourage teachers to do the same.

Map

Invite children to mark their homes on a large map of their community—either for the entire Sunday School, or by department, grade, or class. Also let them mark well-known landmarks (schools, parks, shopping centers, etc.). Such a map can be used throughout the year for such things as:

- ✦ encouraging out-of-class contacts and friendships among children who live in the same areas;
- ✦ adding new children to your group;
- ✦ comparing known distances with those of Bible places;
- ✦ emphasizing that the church is people, not a building.

Class VIP

P.23
Reproducible

1. Choose a different child as VIP for the week.

2. Notify the child and parent ahead of time and ask for something to be brought to class (favorite treat, short book, poster displaying pictures of family, pet, etc.).

3. Send home a flier with students announcing the current VIP (a great interest catcher to combine with announcements of upcoming lessons, activities, Bible verses, etc.).

4. Provide a special name tag for the VIP to wear.

5. Take a few minutes to interview the VIP during a large group time:
- ✦ When is your birthday?
- ✦ What is your favorite snack?
- ✦ What is one of the best books you've ever read?
- ✦ What do you most like to do after you get home from school?

Follow-up/ Attendance Suggestions

PP.25-31
Reproducible

Try some of these ideas to follow up on visitors, absentees and even regular attenders.

1. Send a postcard (see pages 25-31 in this chapter).

2. Ask a supportive parent to call

another parent and affirm that child's attendance. ("My daughter Angie was sure happy that Kamie was in her Sunday School class this week. We've been so pleased with what Angie has been learning in that class. It will be great if Kamie can keep on coming.")

3. Mail or deliver your Sunday School paper to absentees. Send a few left-over copies of previous weeks' papers to new visitors, with a note saying that you hope children will enjoy working on the papers and that they will show some of the things the class has done.

4. Bring a tape recorder, several blank cassettes and a book of riddles to class. As children leave, invite them to record a greeting and read a riddle or two onto the tape to be sent to a child who was not there. Before you mail or deliver the tape, record your own brief greeting. You may also record a brief summary of the class activities. Ask the child to bring the tape the next time he or she comes to class. "Then you can help us record some more greetings and riddles to send to someone who couldn't be here that Sunday."

5. Send home a class roster ("Friends at Class") with names, schools, addresses and phone numbers for all children. Attach a note to the parents encouraging them to help their child build friendships with some of the children in the class. ("We believe positive church experiences involve far more than the organized events and programs we attend. Encouraging the growth of positive relationships with others in the church family is one of the greatest benefits you can provide for your child.")

6. Mail an intriguing item to students for them to bring back the following week. For example:

✦ Link of a paper chain (with child's name on it). Links of a certain color could designate a class or department. Display the completed chain in a prominent location in your church building. Include a note with each link encouraging the child to "help make the longest chain possible!"

✦ Paper leaf. Attach leaves to a tree display on a large bulletin board. Tell children "Let's see if we can fill up the branches on the tree in our classroom."

✦ Jigsaw puzzle pieces to put together in each class or department. Choose Bible, scenic or animal puzzles with approximately 15-20 pieces for elementary age classes and approximately 8-12 pieces for preschool classes.

✦ Music note (with a word below it or a number on the back). Before class, notes are mounted in correct order on a large piece of paper to produce a song.

7. Ask students to bring an item to class. For example:

✦ Piece of fruit. Teachers and kids make a fruit salad to eat at the end of class.

✦ Nature item (leaf, rock, shell, etc.) to be part of a classroom nature display.

✦ Baby picture. Teacher collects and displays pictures. Students try to identify each picture.

Name Tags

PP. 33-35 Reproducible

Name tags are of great value in any children's ministry, reminding teachers and other volunteers to frequently call each child by name. When a child is greeted by name, that child's sense of identity is strengthened; he or she builds positive feelings about being in Sunday School. And that child is more likely to be receptive to the learning experiences. As children begin learning to read, name tags help them learn the names of others in the class. (Most teachers are appalled to discover how few children in a once-a-week program learn the names of more than a few others in their group.)

If you do not use name tags on a regular basis, consider their added value at such times as:

✦ starting a new class;
✦ promotion Sunday;
✦ special events (theme days) and class parties when visitors are expected.

To make name tags, photocopy onto blank labels the art provided on pages 33-35 in this chapter. Letter each child's name on a tag. Or, photocopy the art onto paper, cut tags apart and put them in plastic holders for kids to wear. You may pin or tape paper tags directly onto clothing if tags will not be used again.

Cooperative Contests

Cooperative competition sounds like a contradiction. However, it is one of the best ways to build enthusiasm in a group of children. Traditional competition (someone wins and someone loses) poses real problems in Sunday School where we want EVERY child to be a winner. When individual performance is the basis for "winning," many children quickly give up or never even try, because they know there are others in the group with whom they cannot compete. Also, in many cases (e.g., attendance or Bible memory contests), the child is really being rewarded for effort made by parents, leaving some children with no hope of success.

Cooperative contests engage the entire class or department in reaching a goal, with everyone sharing in the rewards. For example, a cooperative contest might set a class goal for total number of children attending over a period of time, or a total number of Bible verses to be learned. When the goal is reached, the class may be given a special treat or party.

Cooperative contests work well because everyone feels a part, enthusiasm builds as progress towards the goal is measured, there is a certainty of success (if the goal is reasonable), and a shared sense of accomplishment which builds a sense of belonging.

It is wise to set a small goal at first, over a short period of time. When that goal is met, increase the goal, the time length and the reward.

While points can be awarded for a great many things, choose something for which your group needs an incentive in order to improve. Among the activities for which you may give points:

✦ attendance;
✦ bringing Bible;
✦ Bible memory (To avoid discouraging those for whom memorization is difficult, those who are new, and those who get no help at home, you may give credit for saying the verse

in their own words.);
+ bringing a friend;
+ following directions.

There is no limit to the ways in which points can be recorded on a bulletin board display or a large sheet of poster board. Here are a few suggestions:

Rainbow
Use construction paper to make a large rainbow. Cut apart the rainbow and give small sections to children as they earn points. Children add sections to display until the rainbow is complete.

Garden
Make flower petals from white construction paper. As they earn points, children color the petals and add them to a display to form flowers.

Tree
Cut a tree outline from brown construction paper or brown grocery bags and attach it to bulletin board or poster board. Children add paper leaves or fruit to the tree as they earn points.

Kite
Children tie yarn bows onto the string tail of a paper kite. Each yarn bow represents a certain number of points earned. Hang the kite from the ceiling of your room.

Balloons
Children add paper balloons to a display as points are earned.

Happy Faces
Children add happy face stickers to a display.

Paper Chain
Cut construction paper strips. Children link the strips to make a chain with each link representing a point earned.

Similar displays may be formed with Bible story objects. For example, in studying Creation, children may add stars to a sky background. Or, in studying stories of Joseph, draw a large pyramid on poster board. Divide the pyramid into sections. Children color sections to represent points earned.

Poster Contest
PP.37-43 Reproducible

Give every child a doodle-art type poster. Children color the posters (either during the session or at home during the week). Or, ask children to draw posters advertising their Sunday School class. Suggest several slogans or sentence starters children may use ("First Grade Is Fabulous!" "Join Our Juniors—We Keep the Joint Jumping!"). Display completed posters throughout the church facility. Offer a small prize to everyone who participates.

Awards
PP.45-51 Reproducible

Awards have long been a fun way to motivate children (at least those who felt they had a chance). To avoid having children try to defeat each other and result in creating a group of "losers," offer individual awards in ways that ensure every child can be a winner.

Award Tickets
One effective approach is to give award tickets for specific, predetermined actions (e.g., attendance, repeating the Bible verse, bringing

a Bible, or any desired positive behavior—following directions, working on student worksheet, locating a Bible reference, etc.). At the end of the session (or month), award tickets can be exchanged for prizes. Distributing award tickets for positive behavior allows the teacher to make sure everyone gets something. It also is an effective device for reinforcing positive classroom behavior and minimizing disruptive actions.

Bible Memory Awards
While cooperative contests are very effective in getting everyone involved in Bible memory, some students may need an extra incentive to go beyond the minimum. If you offer individual awards to students for Bible memory, consider these guidelines:

1. Avoid a public display which will show how far ahead (or behind) some students are. Unless all students are progressing at close to the same rate, record each student's efforts in a book or folder.

2. Avoid focusing only on recitation which can often be done with little or no understanding. Encourage those who recite to either answer a question about the verse or rephrase the verse in their own words. Allow children for whom memorization is difficult to say the verse in their own words or explain the meaning of the verse.

3. Give ample opportunity for students to review memory work in class before reciting, so that those with no parental support can participate.

4. If children seem to be forgetting the verses almost as quickly as they recite them, require that a verse be recited on two separate

Sundays. After the first recitation, instruct the child to keep reviewing the verse during the week in order to be able to say it from memory the following week.

Attendance Certificates

PP. 53-55
Reproducible

Give every child a certificate for attendance at various special occasions:
✦ Promotion Sunday or the end of the school year;
✦ at the end of a month of perfect attendance;
✦ after a period of special attendance promotion.

Be aware that some children's attendance patterns are influenced by circumstances beyond their control. Plan your attendance awards in such a manner that no child will be left out. For example, give a certificate after five Sundays of attendance, whether they are consecutive or not.

Class Parties

PP. 57-59
Reproducible

Whatever the age of the children, a social event outside of Sunday morning has great benefits:
✦ Children associate Sunday School with having a good time.
✦ Children, teachers and parents get better acquainted.
✦ Children are more likely to invite a friend to an outside event.
✦ Interest can be rekindled among absentees and irregulars.

Consider these tips in organizing the event:

1. Schedule the party well in advance.

2. Check to see if permission slips are needed.

3. Publicize the event well in advance and repeatedly. (Most people need to see or hear a message several times in order to remember it.)

4. Invite parents to assist you. Even if you feel it will be easier to do it yourself, there is great value in working with a few parents, helping them to become better acquainted with you and each other.
Some favorite party ideas include:
✦ picnic/BBQ;
✦ pizza (at a home, at church or at a restaurant);
✦ swimming;
✦ ice skating or roller skating;
✦ roller blading;
✦ biking;
✦ beach;
✦ sports events at a park;
✦ browsing and eating a snack at the local mall (great for older girls);
✦ making ice cream sundaes;
✦ cookie baking.

Sunday School Names

PP. 61-63
Reproducible

Inviting a child to Sunday School is often made difficult by the ordinariness of the name—and what red-blooded, active child wants to go to school on a weekend? Many

churches have found it helpful to rename their Sunday morning program for children, both as a means of reducing negative response to the traditional name and to focus more directly on what the goals and methods of the program really entail. A few names that have proven popular are:
✦ KIDSPACE;
✦ TNT Club (Teachin' Time);
✦ Life Time;
✦ Bible Adventure Hour;
✦ Super Sunday;
✦ Prime Time for Kids;
✦ Kid Connection;
✦ Kidventure;
✦ The Carpenter Shop;
✦ KIDS Club;
✦ Discovery Time.

Sample lettering for these names is provided on pages 61-63 in this chapter. Use appropriate art with this lettering to make posters, membership cards, registration forms, bulletin/newsletter inserts, letterhead, teacher notepads, name tags, etc.

Frequently communicate the reason for your name, keeping children, parents, leaders and the congregation aware of what your children's ministry is aiming to accomplish. For example—

Sunday Morning is Prime Time for Kids because...
✦ Childhood years are a Prime Time of life!
✦ Sunday morning is the Prime Time of the week!

Chapter 7 contains some additional suggestions on ways to communicate to the congregation the goals and emphases of your renamed Sunday School. (See the "Printed and Verbal Announcements" section in chapter 7 on page 183.)

Picture Day

Donut Day

Crazy Hat Day

Video Day

We're glad you came!

we missed YOU!

Welcome to our Sunday School

FREE TICKET!

To: _Sunday School_

Time: _____

Place: _____

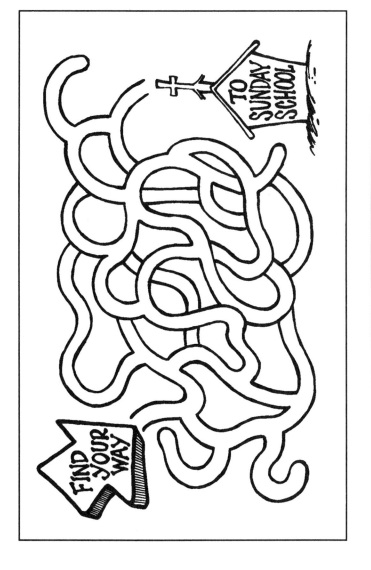

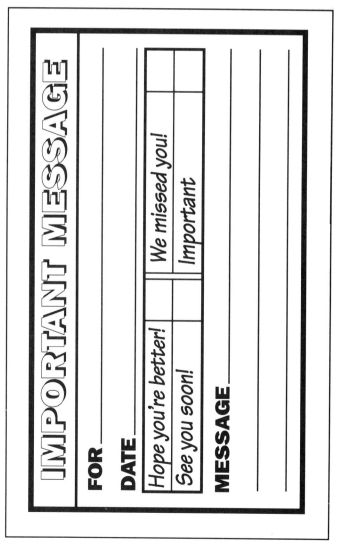

SUNDAY SCHOOL

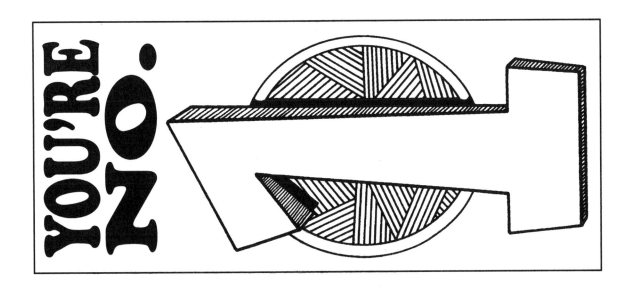

MEMORY CERTIFICATE

To _____

For _____

_____

_____

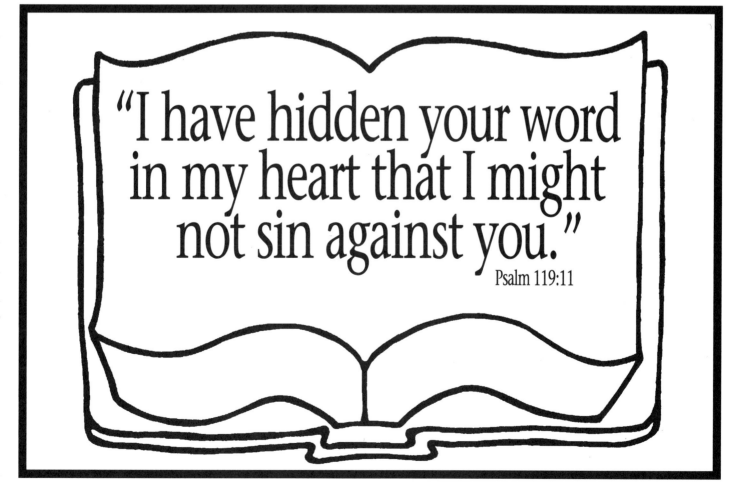

"I have hidden your word in my heart that I might not sin against you."

Psalm 119:11

Attendance Award

We're glad you came!

Attendance Award

Certificate of Attendance

_____

ICE CREAM PARTY

PIZZA PARTY

COME TO THE PICNIC

SWIMMING PARTY

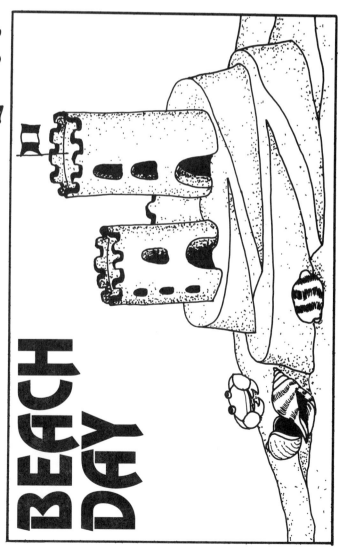

KID CONNECTION

KIDVENTURE!

The Carpenter Shop

DISCOVERY TIME

KIDS

Promote to Parents

"I don't know why Ricky doesn't want to come to church anymore," said the father of a middle schooler. "After all these years, he says he doesn't have any friends in his youth class."

At this point I felt it would have been rubbing salt in this dad's wounds to point out that his family's longtime pattern of sporadic attendance had been a significant factor in Ricky's inability to build strong relationships within the church family. While the parents felt very comfortable coming sometimes to the early service, sometimes to the later one, and sometimes not at all, Ricky always felt like an outsider growing up in his own church.

Many parents who would feel terrible about "letting the team down" if their child skipped a practice or game, who would consider themselves wasteful to miss a music lesson for which they have paid, will not even blink an eye when they plan family activities which pull their child away from Sunday School. "So, he misses hearing about Jonah and the Ark, or doesn't color another picture of David in the lions' den," one less-than-knowledgeable parent asserted. "One Bible story more or less won't make much difference 10 years from now."

Sadly, churches have not always excelled at educating parents about the deep, lasting value of Sunday School. This chapter provides some ideas and resources to use in helping parents understand

what your Sunday School provides for their child. By adopting and adapting these tools, you can positively influence many parents, both inside and outside your church family, to realize the importance for every child of regular attendance at Sunday School.

Bulletin/ Newsletter Inserts

PP.71-75 Reproducible

Every month or so, reproduce one of the inserts provided in this chapter for use in your church bulletin and/or newsletter. (Also see inserts found on pages 187-191 in chapter 7.) To gain maximum impact from these inserts—

1. Always add information about something specific that is going on in your children's Sunday School, including the time, place and age groups involved. (Never assume that everyone knows all that. The only people who really know it are the ones already coming. If you want to attract new people, give them the information they need.)

2. Repeat use of the same insert. People need more than one exposure to a message. Many advertisers claim it takes more than a dozen impressions to move the average person to action.

3. Reduce or enlarge the same insert (with your program information added) for use on:
✦ postcards or letters to parents;
✦ handouts for parents when they drop off or pick up their child;
✦ enclosures in packets for church visitors and/or new members;
✦ posters to display on church and community bulletin boards;
✦ take-home notices for children to give to parents, etc.

Open House

P.77 Reproducible

A Sunday School open house is one of the best ways to acquaint parents with the value of Sunday School for their child. An open house also is a great way for teachers and parents to get to know one another, building bonds of mutual support for the benefit of the child.

One of the most valuable things to do at open house is to let parents observe a class in action. This may be done during the regular Sunday School hour, having parents sit in—and even participate with—their child's own class. Or, if your facility and/or schedule does not allow for a Sunday morning open house, it may be held at another time. Plan to have parents observe a special demonstration class (live or on video).

In addition to the classroom

observation, there is great variety of activities which may be included, depending on your purpose and the time available:

✦ refreshments (essential for helping people relax and mingle);

✦ a brief talk by your pastor, Christian education director or a church member who can effectively articulate the benefits of your Sunday School;

✦ helpful tips for parents on ways to help their child gain the most from Sunday School and other church experiences;

✦ puppet presentation (see pages 193-195 in chapter 7 for additional puppet skits);

✦ musical and/or dramatic presentation by some of the children.

SAMPLE OPEN HOUSE SCHEDULE
Sunday Morning 9:30-10:30

9:30 WELCOME
Greeters/teachers guide parents and children to classes. Children and parents work together in typical learning activities.
Teachers informally guide activities, getting acquainted with parents.

9:40 GROUP TIME
Teacher leads children and parents in singing, Bible Verse activities and Bible Story.

9:55 REFRESHMENTS
Parents move to a separate room for refreshments and conversation.

10:05 PRESENTATION
Puppet/music/drama presentation on value of Sunday School.

10:15 PRESENTATION
Pastor/Director/etc.

10:30 DISMISSAL

Parents return to classroom, look at displays, visit with teacher and pick up child.

Publicize your open house with:

✦ bulletin announcements for several weeks;

✦ flier for kids to take home (mail to absentees);

✦ teachers call parents as a reminder (a great excuse to talk personally with parents teacher does not yet know well).

Tips for Organizing

1. Set the date for your open house far enough ahead so teachers can plan for special displays and appropriate demonstration activities.

2. If the timing of your open house affects adult Sunday School programs, coordinate your plans with these leaders.

3. Provide extra chairs in the rooms to accommodate parents as well as children.

4. Provide name tags for all teachers, students and parents. (See pages 33-35 in chapter 2.)

5. Put up classroom signs if you do not already have them.

6. Enlist extra greeters.

7. Suggest pastoral staff come also to meet parents who don't normally attend church services.

8. Arrange for refreshments to be available.

9. Encourage teachers to drop a note or phone parents who attended to thank them for their interest and further establish communication channels.

Parent of the Week

Invite a different parent to observe/participate in class each week or the first Sunday of each month. (If a parent is unable to attend, suggest the child invite another family member or adult friend.) Several strong benefits are gained from this:

✦ Parents learn a great deal about the value of Sunday School.

✦ Parents pick up tips on ways to communicate better with their own child at home.

✦ Parents and teachers get to know each other better.

✦ Not only do children enjoy having parents in their room, but the presence of a parent makes the class more important to the child.

✦ As children get used to having parents in the room, misbehavior actually diminishes.

✦ The parent may enjoy the observation so much that he or she may want to become involved as a Sunday School teacher.

Tips for Incorporating a Parent into the Classroom

1. If the parent has been invited to observe:

✦ Place a comfortable chair where the parent can see and hear.

✦ Provide copies of any lesson materials.

✦ Arrange for the parent to arrive a few minutes early and remain a few minutes after the session so parent and teacher have opportunity to talk about the session.

✦ Request that the parent not initiate interaction with children, but explain that if a child approaches the parent, it is perfectly all right for the parent to respond, then gently guide the child back towards the class activity.

✦ Alert the parent that his or her child may not behave typically with a parent in the room (e.g., young children may cling to the parent, or a child may show off, etc.).

✦ Introduce the parent to the children and provide an opportunity for the parent and child to share a few photos or items reflecting interests of their family.

✦ Afterwards, invite suggestions from the parent on ways to make the class more interesting for his or her child.

2. If the parent has been invited to assist:

✦ Books or puzzles are excellent "low-threat" activities for a parent volunteer to lead with young children, as long as the teacher carefully selects the books and puzzles.

✦ With elementary-aged children, first-time parent volunteers tend to work best assisting a teacher with an activity rather than leading an activity on their own.

✦ Parents who have specific talents or interests (music, cooking, carpentry, art, etc.) can often use that ability in a lesson-related activity.

To publicize the Parent of the Week plan, send home a note inviting parents to select a first, second and third choice for the date to visit. Follow up with those who do not respond. A week before the parent is to come, make a reminder phone call or send a postcard. Invite the parent to bring a few family photos and/ or an item or two reflecting a special interest of their family. And by all means, remind the child that his or her parent is "Parent of the Week."

Parent Memo

P.79 Reproducible

Duplicate a quantity of this memo form. Give copies to every teacher to write personal notes and mail to parents, telling something that went on in class, something their child said, a current topic of study, etc.

Teachers may use the memos:
✦ when a child has recently joined the Sunday School class;
✦ when a child has had a difficult time participating (separation or discipline problems, shyness, boredom, etc.);
✦ when a child had a particularly good time in class or exhibited improvement in some area;
✦ when a child said something insightful, funny or cute;
✦ when a child showed particular interest in a topic.

Suggest teachers set up a schedule so a different child's parent gets a memo each week.

Parent Feedback

P.81 Reproducible

Duplicate copies of this form for teachers to send or mail to parents as a means of encouraging parent communication with teachers. Feedback can help teachers learn what works or doesn't work with specific children. It also gives parents a means of expressing their ideas, helping them feel a part of Sunday School. The feedback form also encourages parents and children to talk together about Sunday School. Parents may

place their completed forms in a box by the front door of the classroom, or by mailing forms directly to the teacher.

Seasonal Ideas

PP.81-85 Reproducible

Holiday times are natural opportunities to contact parents. Parents are often looking for ways to help their children experience the spiritual significance of such holidays as Christmas and Easter. Some parents need to be reminded that Sunday School is one of the best ways to help a child discover and enjoy the rich meaning of the holiday.

Reproduce the reminders provided in this chapter (see pages 83-85) on letters or postcards sent directly to inform parents of what the Sunday School is doing for the holiday. Also place the reminders in the church bulletin and newsletter. Along with the reminders, add your own program information about the place and time of Sunday School, names of teachers, special seasonal events coming for various family members—women's or men's events, parenting workshops ("Surviving the Gimme Syndrome," "Holidays and Families: Drawing Together or Pulling Apart?"), all-church events, schedule changes, etc.

Brochures

PP.87-91 Reproducible

A simple but attractive brochure about your Sunday School (or total children's ministry program) is a helpful tool to give to visitors, parents and/or new members on special occasions or throughout the year. A good brochure includes:

✦ age/grade ranges, times and locations of classes;

✦ information about leaders and teachers (Listing names is nice, but it can outdate the brochure in a hurry; describing the general qualities and qualifications of staff is generally best for a brochure.);

✦ a general statement of purpose for the program, written to appeal to parents not yet fully committed to your church's ministries. (The people who are already committed don't need the brochure, so avoid in-group jargon that may put off the people you are trying to reach.)

You may also include:

✦ eye-catching headlines (see pages 235-237 in chapter 8);

✦ a brief description of the types of activities provided for children;

✦ pictures of classes in action;

✦ quotes from children telling why they like to come.

Tips for an Appealing Brochure

✦ Include graphics: art done by children, clip art (see pages 87-91 in this chapter and pages 213-217 in chapter 8), a map of the campus.

✦ Include a theme Bible verse, such as "Let the little children come to me" (Mark 10:14), "Train a child in the way he should go" (Proverbs 22:6), or "A little child will lead them" (Isaiah 11:6).

✦ Limit the amount of copy. Too many words will stop readers before they get started.

Sample Brochure

front

First Church
9999 Broadway
Main City

659-3333

Rev. John Doe,
Pastor

Mrs. Lois Stevens,
Children's Director

Preschool
688-4232
Jean Smith,
Director

"Let the little children come to me."
Mark 10:14

First Church

A Special Place for Your Child to Learn and Grow

back

Let Your Children Come

✦ to build friendships within our church family,
✦ to enjoy the personal concern of teachers who care,
✦ to learn the good news of God's love as shown through Jesus Christ,
✦ to "grow in wisdom and in stature and in favor with God and people" (see Luke 2:52).

We invite your child to be part of the following programs

Sunday Mornings	Special Events	Music
✦Sunday School for all ages at 9:45 A.M.	✦Vacation Bible School meets the last week in June.	✦Children's Choir meets Mondays at 3:30 P.M.
Babies — Nursery 2s & 3s — Room 2 4s & 5s — Room 4	✦Advent Night is the first Sunday in December.	✦Preschool Choir meets Thursdays at 3:00 P.M.

inside

Registration Sundays

Annual registration is a great excuse to promote the value of Sunday School to parents and the congregation. It also allows you to be sure you have current information on children and their families. The main benefits, however, are that parents tend to take something more seriously if they have to sign up for it, and many will be jogged by this action to commit to improving their child's attendance pattern.

Select one or more Sundays and actively promote them as the days on which children are to be registered. (Fall is a great time to have parents register their child for the coming Sunday School year.) Set up one or more registration tables where people tend to congregate after Sunday School and worship services. Have registration cards for parents to complete. (OPTION: Mail registration cards to parents for them to bring already filled in.) Also have copies of your brochure and one or more articles of interest to parents. Staff the tables with friendly, outgoing people who are familiar enough with your program to answer questions correctly. (Having teachers at the tables is a good way of identifying for the congregation who your teachers are.) Provide attractive name tags for those at the tables.

Throughout the year, have registration materials available for new parents to complete. By extending a friendly invitation to "sign Johnny up for the rest of the year," greeters or secretaries can play a big role in helping parents step over the line from being "casual visitors" to feeling they are part of the church family.

Articles for Parents

PP. 93-99
Reproducible

Several brief, informative articles for parents are included on pages 93-99 in this chapter. These—or other appropriate articles for which you obtain permission to reproduce—can be used in a variety of ways to aid parents and build their awareness of the Sunday School as a resource agency which is ready to benefit them.

✦ Periodically arrange for teachers to send or mail these home, including a personal note about the child or the class.

✦ Place articles by entrance to children's rooms.

✦ Distribute articles at open house or when parents register for the new school year.

Some things were meant to be difficult...

Some things were *not!*

Learning about God's Word can be a "puzzling" experience for children. Our Sunday School is designed to help young learners put all the pieces together. Each week, caring teachers lead children in Bible study, music and creative activities. Sunday School helps your child take the guesswork out of Bible learning and everyday living in our complex world.

HERE'S WHY SO MANY PARENTS BRING THEIR KIDS TO SUNDAY SCHOOL:

Because the teachers genuinely care about each child.

Because children learn how Bible truths make a difference in their lives.

Because children need friends who are a part of God's family.

Because children enjoy the variety of creative learning activities.

And, because parents get so much out of the adult ministries our church provides at the same time.

IMPORTANT MESSAGE

FOR: _Parents of Children_

DATE: _Today_   TIME: _9:00_A.M.

FROM: _Sunday School Teachers_

Would like to see your child	X	Will call again	
Returning your call		URGENT	X

MESSAGE: _Your child is invited to attend Sunday School, the place for making friends and learning how God's love makes every day better!_

At Sunday School we'll get your kids into the Bible, so your kids can get the Bible into their lives.

Sunday School — using a 1st-century Book to prepare today's kids for 21st-century life!

In the changing world of children, one thing remains rock solid...

THE VALUE OF SUNDAY SCHOOL!

DON'T LET YOUR CHILD'S FAITH MELT AWAY.

Sunday School is a special opportunity for children to grow in their relationship to God and other Christians.

What Are Your Kids Under the Influence of?

☐ **Their Friends**   ☐ **Television**   ☐ **The Comics**   ☐ **The Bible**

In today's complex world, kids encounter struggles that we probably never experienced. Struggles that require them to make important choices much earlier. That's why kids need to be getting into the Bible — as early as possible! Our Sunday School will familiarize your kids with the Bible. They'll be learning about Jesus Christ. Learning about life. Learning about real people who followed God in Bible times. And most importantly, learning how to use their own Bibles, so they can get the Bible into their lives.

Plant the Seeds of Faith in Your Child at Sunday School.

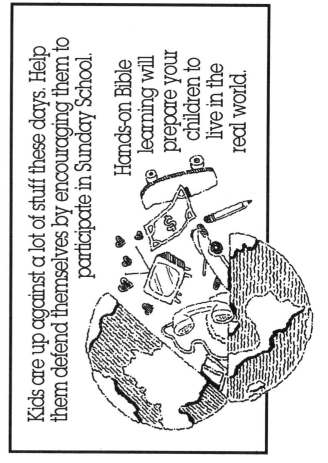

Kids are up against a lot of stuff these days. Help them defend themselves by encouraging them to participate in Sunday School.

Hands-on Bible learning will prepare your children to live in the real world.

Hey, Mom and Dad!
You're invited to come with me to
SUNDAY SCHOOL OPEN HOUSE

We're gonna have a great time together and I really want you to come!
You get to come to my class and eat goodies and talk to my teacher and
eat goodies and.... Anyway, you get the idea. And my teachers promise
not to tell you anything bad about me. So, please come with me next Sunday.

Your Loving and Intelligent Child,

Welcome to Open House!

Observation Notes

	Yes	No
1. Did you hear a child spoken to individually and called by name?	☐	☐
2. Did you hear a teacher praise a particular action by a child?	☐	☐
3. Did you hear a child's negative feelings being understood by a teacher?	☐	☐
4. Did you hear a teacher relate a positive attitude or action to a Bible concept?	☐	☐
5. Did you hear a child's ideas accepted even if not entirely correct?	☐	☐
6. Did you hear a teacher correct a child in a positive way?	☐	☐

If not, please let us know. We want to keep improving in the ways we show God's love to your child.

S M T W T F S

 Parent of the Week

Who: YOU!
What: Come to Sunday School next week!
When:
Where:

Why: To observe your child's class — a great way to see your child in action with a group of friends, to notice ways in which we seek to help your child learn — AND TO SHOW YOUR CHILD YOU SUPPORT THE VALUE OF LEARNING IN SUNDAY SCHOOL!

MEMO

To: _____

From: _____

Date: _____

_____
_____
_____
_____

PLEASE LET US KNOW!

Please complete this form and return it to your child's Sunday School teacher. Thank you.

Child _____ Parent _____

As a parent, I would like Sunday School to _____

At Sunday School my child most enjoys _____

My child's least favorite activity is _____

My child wishes that Sunday School would _____

☐ Allergies/Special Needs: _____

More or Less

NEW YEAR'S RESOLUTIONS

1. Smile more!
2. Eat less.
3. Exercise more!
4. Frown less.
5. Bring my child to Sunday School more!
6. Be absent less.

Does Easter Mean Beans to Your Kids?

If you agree that Easter should do more for your children than raise their blood sugar level, we invite you and your family to celebrate the miracle of Easter.

When: _____

Where: _____

Better Than Bunnies!

Don't Neglect the 3 R's

Religion, Relationships and Rejoicing!

Hi!

Back to Sunday School

No more pencils, no more School! Twelve whole weeks to play it **Cool!**

Betcha our parents will be happy we're finally home on vacation!

Is Something Missing?

★ Christmas to Do List
- ☐ Mail cards
- ☐ Buy gifts
- ☐ Select tree
- ☐ Decorate house
- ☐ Bake cookies
- ☐ Wrap gifts
- ☐ Visit Aunt Edna
- ☐ Christmas Party

★ Put Sunday School at the top of the list!

Sunday School

The place to be this Christmas

"Ring in the season" at Sunday School!

"Let the little children come to me."

Mark 10:14

A Special Place for Your Child to Learn and Grow

Let Your Children Come

♦ to build friendships within our church family,
♦ to enjoy the personal concern of teachers who care,
♦ to learn the good news of God's love
   as shown through Jesus Christ,
♦ to "grow in wisdom and in stature and
   in favor with God and people" (see Luke 2:52).

We invite your child to be part of the following programs

Sunday Mornings	Special Events	Music

**"Train a child
in the way he
should go."**
Proverbs 22:6

Sunday School

Time: Place:

For More Information:

"A little child will lead them."

(See Isaiah 11:6.)

Children's Ministries

Childhood Is Not a Disease

"Jesus said, 'Let the little children come to me, and do not hinder them, for the kingdom of heaven belongs to such as these.'"
Matthew 19:14

The most striking thing about Jesus' encounter with these little ones is not that He interrupted an adult meeting to take time for some children. Nor is it surprising that He physically picked up the children and loved them. The remarkable part of this incident is Jesus' words. Most adults would have said something like "Let the little children come to me, and don't prevent them, for some day they will grow up and become important."

Jesus saw something in childhood besides the future. He recognized worth and value in the state of being a child, for He told the waiting adults in this crowd that children are important for what they are right now.

We adults always seem to be looking to the future. This push for preparation robs childhood of much of its essence, as parents and teachers urge little ones hurriedly through the present in search of a more significant future.

The Future Is Now

"I know it's hard for a three-year-old to sit quietly and listen, but I have to start getting him ready for later when he will have to sit still."

"If he's going to be a success in life he'll have to go to college. And to make sure he can stay ahead in school, I'm going to teach him to read before he starts first grade if it kills us both!"

"If a child is going to grow up with an appreciation for the great hymns of the church, you just can't start too young to teach them."

These and many similar statements are used repeatedly by parents and teachers who are earnestly concerned about helping young children get ready for future roles and demands. However, these well-meaning adults sometimes actually do more harm than good, because in their long-range view of growth they have lost sight of the value in just being a child.

Children are more than people in transition, waiting for some future date of real meaning. The qualities that come from being young are not flaws or imperfections. Rather, childhood is a marked and definable stage of development.

"But an adult has so many capabilities and accomplishments far beyond those of a child. Surely the years of productive and responsible adulthood are more significant than those of infancy and early childhood."

What adult experiences could replace the laughter of children that gladdens the hearts of all who hear? How many hours of labor would it take to equal a little girl's smile? What a sterile world this would be were children not present to add their unique joys and sorrows!

The Value of a Child

Has any parent ever seen more deeply into him- or herself than when holding a newborn child and looking into the child's eyes? All the writings and research of humankind couldn't provide the insights that come with reliving the experiences of a child starting out on his or her own unique adventure. The child's fresh enthusiasm for everything seen, the child's honest questions and powerfully simple logic, all combine to peel the scales from our encrusted adult eyes.

What is the value of a child—as a child?
Incalculable!
This is no plea for attempting to stop the progress of maturation.

It is a call to recognize that just because a phase of life is brief, and is replaced by another more sophisticated, we should not rush past it. For if we bypass the unique stages of childhood, we strip each succeeding developmental stage of some of its finest ingredients. The best preparation for any phase of life is the proper completion of the previous one. The second coat of paint must always wait for the first to dry. Harvest never begins when the first green shoots appear in the spring. Human life has an aching void when childhood is squeezed away.

Is this what Jesus had in mind when He took a small child in His arms and said, "I tell you the truth, unless you change and become like little children, you will never enter the kingdom of heaven" (Matthew 18:3). Is there a place in our homes and churches for children to be children? Do we wholeheartedly accept them as they are, not as we wish they were? Do the rooms and materials we provide sound out "Welcome!" to a young learner? Are the adults who surround young children deeply sympathetic and understanding of what these special years are all about?

Or do we merely see little ones in terms of their potential, enduring them until they get old enough to really matter? Is the church's objective in providing children's ministries a means of attracting their parents, or of getting ready for the church of tomorrow? Is our goal to train young children to act like miniature adults because their noisy spontaneity may somehow mar our sacred corridors?

W.C. Fields wrung many laughs from his famous line, "Anyone who hates dogs and kids can't be all bad." But have you ever met a person who wanted to live in a world where everyone shared Field's dislike of children?

It's far better to follow the Lord Jesus' pattern with children. His loving response to the children lets us see into His heart's feeling of the worth of a young life.

Childhood is not a disease to be cured or endured. It is a God-ordained part of human life with value and significance that continually enriches the experiences of those who may have forgotten what it is like to see the world from a fresh, unspoiled point of view.

I Don't Wanna Go to Sunday School

"Everybody ought to go to Sunday School, Sunday School, Sunday School. The mothers and the fathers and the boys and the girls, everybody ought to go to Sunday School."

When you read the words of this old-time chorus, what images come to your mind? A happy mother and father with 1.2 children cheerfully walking up the steps to church? A mother single-handedly struggling to get her children to the church on time? A continuing argument with a rebellious child who declares each week, "Sunday School is bor-r-r-ing"?

No matter what your situation, there is bound to be a time when you, as a parent, come face-to-face with a child's reluctance to attend Sunday School. For parents, it may start in the early years as you pry the clinging arms of a toddler from around your neck or listen to wails of despair as you hurriedly make your exit from the church nursery. Later on, as your child grows, you wonder how to respond when your son or daughter unexpectedly asks, "Can't we just stay home this week?" Sunday School teachers, too, feel moments of despair and frustration when they sense some children's unwilling attendance in their classes.

So, who's going to Sunday School? Everybody! And here are some guidelines for how you can make it happen in your family or class.

Don't Panic!

When you first hear the screams, complaints or questions, keep in mind that often the best approach is a light touch. A parent who threatens a reluctant Sunday School attender with God's disapproval or anger runs the risk of making a mountain out of the proverbial molehill. A matter-of-fact response will usually solve the problem. For example, a parent might answer, "In our family we always plan to go to Sunday School. You know, one thing I really like about Sunday School is getting to see some of my friends. Who is one of your friends at Sunday School?" Turning a negative complaint into a positive statement is a way to increase your child's enthusiasm for Sunday School. At some point, with an older child, a firm approach might be needed. "I know you would rather not attend Sunday School right now. But I think going to Sunday School is a really good way to keep learning about God and how He wants us to live. So we'll keep going to Sunday School."

Take Action

There are several ways in which parents can work to build a child's enthusiasm for Sunday School. If your child does not attend the same school as others in his or her class or has just recently begun attending Sunday School, plan some get-acquainted times to help your child feel more comfortable in class. Invite another child and his or her family over for an informal dinner or a picnic in the park. It might even be helpful to ask your child's teacher over for dessert. Let your child know you are interested in what happens in his or her class. Ask to see your child's completed Sunday School worksheets. Take time to talk about them; memorize the Bible verses together. Before Sunday School, pray together asking God to help each one in your family enjoy a time of learning and worship at church.

Parents may find that sometimes a child may not enjoy Sunday School due to factors which cannot be changed. Your child may be the only girl in a class of boys or there may be a lack of variety in the class sessions.

In these circumstances, it helps to first acknowledge your child's unhappy feelings. Listen to his or her thoughts about Sunday School. Then you may be able to suggest several ideas to your child. It may be possible for you to help as a volunteer (lead a special activity, help with record keeping, act as greeter, etc.) in the class. Or you and your child may decide to invite the class to your home for a party. Encourage your child to invite a friend to attend class with him or her. Even while acknowledging to your child that the class may not be the most "fun" group in which he or she has been involved, it's important to focus on the positive rather than the negative factors.

Be an Example

It probably doesn't surprise you to learn that the greatest influence on a child's attitude toward Sunday School is the attitude and actions of the adults in the child's life. Your decisions as a parent are signals to your child about the importance of Sunday School. A pattern of consistency in attendance and positive statements about the benefits of Sunday School will do more to affect your child's participation than anything else.

Parents who demonstrate their own enjoyment of Sunday School and exhibit a caring attitude toward their child's needs and feelings will be more likely to find a positive response in their children. Let your enthusiasm for Sunday School overflow into the lives of your children.

Teaching Young Children About God

Young children are curious. They are especially curious about God. They are curious about where He lives, what He wears, how He does things and when He will answer their latest prayer request. Because they are curious about God, they pick up many different things they hear and see, and early in life they form very definite ideas and feelings about Him.

Christian parents have the responsibility to provide young children with healthy guidance that will satisfy their curiosity. The best place to begin this process is for parents and teachers to consider the instructions of Moses.

The book of Deuteronomy shows Moses as an old man, standing before the nation of Israel. He is nearing the end of his career and his life. He knows that in a short time he will be gone and the people will finally enter the Promised Land.

What can Moses tell these people to ensure that their children do not forget all God has done? What system can Moses initiate that can effectively communicate God's laws and God's love?

Early in his message to Israel, Moses gave the clearest instructions in Scripture for introducing God into a child's life:

"Love the Lord your God
with all your heart
and with all your soul
and with all your strength.
These commandments
that I give you today
are to be upon your hearts.
Impress them on your children.

Talk about them
when you sit at home
and when you walk
along the road,
when you lie down
and when you get up."
(Deuteronomy 6:5-7)

1. Model Your Love for God

Moses started with the most important step. Teaching about God is first of all the process of being an example of God in everyday life. Moses told us to focus on loving God before trying to teach about God.

How can a parent communicate love for God in ways a young child can understand?

✦ **Talk about God around the child.** Do your children hear you talking about God with other adults? Do you give God enough of your attention that He is part of your patterns of thought and speech—even when you are not specifically trying to "teach" the child something?

✦ **Use your own Bible.** Before you start reading the Bible to your children, make sure they know you read it yourself. A book that you are interested in is a book they will want to learn about.

✦ **Use Christian music.** Records and tapes are great, but your own voice lifted in praise is far better. The melodies and rhymes of songs have an impact far beyond the words alone. And your enjoyment of the music makes its appeal even greater—whether you sing well or not!

✦ **Pray with children.** Pray naturally, simply and briefly about the things that interest children. Talking to God about scraped knees and other "minor" events conveys that God is interested.

✦ **Demonstrate hospitality.** Mel Howell, one of the pastors at the Evangelical Free Church in Fullerton, California, says, "Many aspects of the Christian life are better caught than taught. Christ calls us to demonstrate our love for Him by extending love and care to others." Many activities in Sunday School and at home provide a wealth of opportunity for children to observe and practice caring for others.

✦ **Build relationships.** As a parent demonstrates love and care for the child, the child develops the capacity to respond to the love and care of the heavenly Father. Gentle touch, warmth in the voice, eye-to-eye conversation and careful listening are all

learned skills that adults need to develop in order to nourish the child's need for love.

2. Teach Diligently

Next Moses called for diligent teaching. This is not a hobby or an occasional pursuit. Moses knew that God would only become important in the life of a child if parents and teachers consistently presented Him to the child.

The first question many parents ask is about WHAT they are to teach. While there is much the young child cannot comprehend about God, there are many concepts that the child can grasp and that contribute to the child's healthy spiritual growth:

✦ God created all things.

✦ God loves everyone.

✦ God sent Jesus.

✦ Jesus died, but lives today.

✦ God forgives me.

The list goes on, with the child's capacity for understanding growing as the child is surrounded by loving instruction from parents and teachers. Here are a few good rules of thumb in making WHAT you teach meaningful to a young child:

Keep it brief—
attention spans are short.

Avoid symbolism—
literal minds are at work.

Ask questions—
let the child tell what he or she liked best about what you said.

Another practical issue of diligent teaching is WHEN to do it. Be alert to situations which can become natural teaching opportunities.

A third issue of diligent teaching is HOW to do it. Consider these tips:

✦ **Use variety.** Books, music and videos are great assets in staying out of a rut. If your resources are limited, check your church, school and local libraries—or arrange a swap with a church family.

✦ **Keep learning life-related.** Focus on concerns the child is facing today. The child needs a sense of God's interest in daily living long before the child needs a chronological understanding of the Bible or a theological definition.

✦ **Keep teaching times brief and simple.** A good rule of thumb is to limit teaching time to one minute for each year of the child's age. Trying to hold the attention of a three-year-old beyond three minutes is stretching, and you run the risk of having the child's interest drop off before you get to the key point you want to emphasize.

✦ **Be flexible.** Be willing to bend to meet the child's needs and interest. The goal is not to get the child to sit still and quit wiggling while the adult talks. The goal is for the adult and child to enjoy being together, learning to love God and each other.

✦ **Talk informally.** The word "teaching" usually brings to mind images of chalkboard, lectures, tests and homework. Perhaps a better word to use when considering God and young children would be "introducing." Think of how you would talk to a child about a dear friend you want the child to know and love. Long discourses are likely to make the child hope that "dear friend" never comes to visit. But brief conversations about that friend can arouse the child's interest.

3. Ask Questions

Perhaps the best way to ensure that the child enjoys these conversations is to ask questions the child can answer.

✦ Which flower (tree, bird, animal, etc.) do you like best? If God has a favorite flower, what do you think it is?

✦ Why do you suppose God made snails (slugs, spiders, ants, etc.)?

✦ Which foods would you like to thank God for? Why do you think God made so many different things for us to eat?

✦ Which person in that story would you like to have for a friend? What makes someone a good friend? Why is Jesus such a good friend?

✦ What do you think might have happened in that story if the people had acted like God wants people to behave?

✦ What happened today that made you feel happy (sad, angry, etc.)? What could you tell God about what happened?

4. Answer Questions

It is not necessary that we be able to answer all the child's questions and fully explain everything about God. It is perfectly all right to point out that there are many things about God that no one knows. Since God is so much greater than any man or woman, there will always be things about Him no one can answer. Honestly admitting what we do not know is far healthier than trying to bluff our way through.

Once the child realizes that even grown-ups are in awe of God's greatness, he or she needs reassurance that, while we cannot know all about God, we can know some very important things about Him. As parents regularly affirm for the child what they do know of God, the child will grow to know Him also.

You Are Vital to Your Child's Sunday School Experience

How to Help Your Child Get the Most Out of Sunday School

1. Encourage your child to develop friendships at Sunday School. One of the strongest benefits the church provides your family is an extended "family" of both adult and childhood friends who support positive Christian values. Consistent attendance makes it easy for meaningful friendships to grow.

2. Be consistent in bringing your child to Sunday School so that he or she will benefit from the biblical instruction. Children are surrounded by influences which are often in conflict with the truths of Scripture. Sunday School can be your child's most important hour out of every week!

3. Cultivate friendships with your child's teachers. It's easier for you to approach two or three teachers than for them to personally contact the parents of all the children in their classes. Your support helps teachers do a good job!

4. Watch for and talk with your child about the take-home materials provided each week. A few minutes of informal conversation at home can help to reinforce and apply the Bible truths your child has studied.

5. Learn the Bible memory verses with your child. Copy each week's verse onto a folded index card and set it on your breakfast table.

6. Ask a few questions about the Bible story to see what your child remembers and understands—and talk about how the story illustrates familiar experiences at home or in the neighborhood. A good question is, "What is one way you can do what that story teaches us?"

7. During the week look for ways to connect a recent Bible verse or story to specific situations. For example, while watching TV, ask how a character's action compares with those of a person in a Bible story.

How to Help Your Child Get the Most Out of Worship Services

1. Enter the worship building as a family, introducing your child to the adults you greet. This helps your child feel like part of the worshiping community.

2. Sit near the front so your child can see easily. Children tend to pay better attention and participate more the closer to the front they sit.

3. Before the service begins, take a few moments with your child to look over the order of worship in the bulletin. Comment on one or two things—unfamiliar or difficult terms, what the child should do at a certain time, why an item is included in worship, what meaning an item has for you.

4. Encourage your child to follow the order of the service. Ask your child to locate and read over the hymns or choruses ahead of time in order to identify unfamiliar words and phrases.

5. Share a hymnal, bulletin and Bible with your child. Holding a book together helps the child to feel a sense of participation.

6. If you are invited to shake hands with people nearby during the worship service, introduce your child to those you greet. Most adults tend to converse over the tops of children's heads, making children feel like outsiders.

7. Each week during the service ask your child to write answers to a question based on the Scripture passage, songs and/or the sermon. Questions might be, "What do you learn about God? What do you learn about how God wants us to act?"

8. After reading Scripture or singing a song, provide pencil and paper for your child to write a one-sentence summary of the Scripture or song. Some children may enjoy drawing pictures to illustrate a song or Scripture passage.

CHAPTER FOUR
Time for Teachers

He was a hospital administrator by profession and a Sunday School teacher by calling. Asked to compare his hospital's volunteer programs with his experience as a teacher at church, he grimaced and said, "If our hospital treated volunteers like our church treats Sunday School teachers, we wouldn't have any volunteers left!"

What are we communicating to Sunday School teachers about the value of their teaching ministry?

✦ "It's a dirty job, but somebody has to do it."

✦ "I feel like I've been given a life sentence in the three-year-old department."

✦ "I suppose that if missionaries are willing to go to Africa, I shouldn't complain about being sent to the Junior class."

✦ "I've learned a lot since I've been teaching. I've learned the meaning of 'burned out.'"

If any of these laments could have come from teachers in your Sunday School, the ideas and resources in this chapter are for you! Even if all your teachers are always happy to be teaching Sunday School, these resources will bolster them. Teachers engaged in Sunday School ministry can never receive too much encouragement and appreciation. You can demonstrate in meaningful ways that your church places a high value on the ministry of teaching children. Also include volunteers who serve in other capacities in your children's ministry.

Thank-you Gifts

At the beginning or end of the teaching term or school year, give a gift to express appreciation to all teachers. Explain that the gift in no way monetarily reimburses the teacher. Instead, it is a symbol or token of gratitude for faithful, excellent service.

Consider these gift ideas:

✦ seasonal items (Christmas ornament, Easter lily);

✦ flowers or potted plants;

✦ personalized mugs, tote bags, T-shirts, pens, pencils, and/or notepads;

✦ books;

✦ food items (fresh fruit, baked goods, preserves, etc.);

✦ gift certificates;

✦ class pictures.

Some gifts (mugs, bags, notepads) can be imprinted, stenciled, patched, or painted with a logo from the church or your children's ministry—or a slogan or theme verse.

Some gifts help identify teachers at church, creating a team spirit—e.g., a tote bag in which to carry supplies.

Thank-you Cards

PP.109-117 Reproducible

At least once or twice during each teacher's term, send a thank-you note or card, providing a tangible expression of gratitude for a job well done.

Often the most appreciated cards are those that kids write and/or illustrate. Younger children enjoy making a book of their own drawings with a special cover. Arranging for children to do this may require a little planning (so the teacher in question is not present when the cards are being made). Children can make cards:

✦ when regular teacher is absent;

✦ while participating in another program—churchtime, midweek, etc.;

✦ at home—requires cooperation from parents;

✦ in the hallway—place poster board and felt pen(s) by classroom door or in the hall near the class. Parents and/or kids may write thank-you notes on it. Letter a starter sentence or two around the border of the poster board.

The "Thank-you Cards" on pages 109-117 in this chapter can be duplicated and used as:

✦ cover pages for a book of children's art—each child may sign his or her name in the blank space;

✦ individual thank-you notes or

cards—you, the children, the parents, the pastor, etc., can write a personal thank-you in each note or card;

✦ thank-you posters—make a transparency of the page; then, using an overhead projector, aim the image onto a sheet of poster board and trace the projected image.

Teacher Interviews

Arrange for your pastor or other "up-front" person to interview one or more teachers during a worship service or in adult Sunday School classes. Carefully select the teachers to be interviewed to accomplish some or all of these purposes:

1. Make all teachers feel appreciated and important.

2. Articulate the purposes and benefits of teaching Sunday School.

3. Uphold people's perception of Sunday School teachers as high-caliber people.

Provide the teachers and interviewer with a brief list of questions to keep the interview on track:

1. How did you get started teaching Sunday School?

2. What do you remember about the first class you taught?

3. What is one of your favorite parts of teaching Sunday School?

4. Why do you still give time and energy to teaching Sunday School?

5. How have you benefitted from being a Sunday School teacher?

Dedication/ Recognition Days

Designate a Sunday at the beginning of the teaching term to dedicate or recognize those who will be teaching in the coming term. There are a variety of ways to do this:

✦ Offer a dedication prayer in the worship service.

✦ Introduce the teachers and other volunteers in the worship service.

✦ List the teachers' names and classes in the bulletin.

✦ Serve special refreshments after church in honor of the teachers who are each given a corsage/boutonniere, button or special name tag to wear.

Teacher of the Month

✦ Hang recognition banners in the entryway or sanctuary.

✦ Select two or three children to share briefly what they like about Sunday School and their teacher. (Have an essay contest with prizes for all entries.)

✦ Include recognition/dedication for people in your church who teach children in school during the week. Affirm your church's support for their Christian witness.

✦ Enlist the pastor or other leader to preach on a related topic—importance of ministry to children, the value of service, the need for teachers, Jesus as a teacher, etc. (After the sermon,

encourage people to become prayer partners with children's teachers. See "Prayer Partners" section on page 205 in chapter 7.)

Whichever approach you take, be sure to alert the teachers ahead of time so they are aware of the plan. If your church has multiple worship services, identify which service each teacher will attend.

Bulletin/ Newsletter Features

PP. 119-121 Reproducible

Feature a different teacher or department each week or month in the bulletin or newsletter. Include personal notes about each teacher using the "Did you know...?" format. Encourage the congregation to pray for these teachers during the coming week/month.

Periodically list the names of teachers in the bulletin or newsletter. Encourage the congregation to thank these people for their effective teaching.

VIP
P. 121 Reproducible

Give teachers a VIP name tag, corsage/boutonniere, pin or badge to wear on a special Sunday (Dedication/Recognition Day, first day of term, etc.). Alert the congregation through pulpit and bulletin announcements that the many VIPs in their midst are teachers of children.

Personal Occasions

Send birthday cards to teachers—and be alert to other special times (job promotion, anniversary, new baby, etc.) in the lives of your teachers. The caring you demonstrate for them will model the caring they should show their children.

Teacher Bulletin Board

Put up a bulletin board in a well-traveled area of the church facility. Feature one department or age level each month, showing individual pictures of teachers with their names and the grade level each one teaches. Include several pictures of teachers in action with their classes.

Vary the headings on this bulletin board from month to month:

"Very Important People"

"Look Who's Teaching Our Kids"

"An Apple for Our Teachers" (over a big apple background)

"The People Who Make Things Happen"

"Touching Tomorrow by Teaching Children"

"Focus on Four- and Five-Year-Olds"

"Terrific Third Grade Teachers"

Teacher Treats

Designate one Sunday as Teacher Treat Day. Ask a parent from each class to bring a basket of muffins or cookies or other treat to the child's teacher with a thank-you card that all children sign. (Option: Parent and child may deliver treats to teacher's home.)

Teacher Recognition Events

Plan an annual event to honor your teachers. Include the teachers and their spouses, family or other guests. Invite people who have served faithfully in the past, but are unable to do so now (or who have been led into other areas of ministry). Or, invite the whole congregation to attend.

There is almost no limit to the kinds of events you could offer:
✦ breakfast, brunch or lunch;
✦ banquet, potluck dinner or dessert;
✦ family picnic, barbecue, pizza party or ethnic feast;
✦ short program after eating or a full evening program with little or no food;
✦ concert, guest speaker, film or video.

The list is endless! These can be major events with decorations, special foods, table centerpieces, and entertainment. Or they can be low-key and informal. The key is

that they be well planned, communicating that someone thinks the teachers are important enough to have gone to some trouble on their behalf.

Consider these tips for making these events successful:
✦ Plan ahead so that people can arrange their schedules and the event can be well organized.
✦ Mail invitations, then follow up with a personal call.
✦ Enlist parents of children and other church members to do as much of the work as possible. The more people that are involved in saying thank-you, the more meaningful the event will be.
✦ Always use name tags, for it is highly unlikely that everyone who comes will know everyone else. (Nonteaching spouses are often reluctant to attend events at which they feel like outsiders.)
✦ Plan a get-acquainted activity that encourages people to mingle and meet each other. (See suggestions later in this chapter.)
✦ Make sure that everyone involved in the program (speaker, pastor, musical group, etc.) understands that the purpose is to encourage and honor the teachers, not to twist their arms to do even more than they've been doing.
✦ If possible and appropriate, show slides or a video of children in their classes.
✦ Plan a joint celebration with a nearby church and their teachers.
✦ Invite former students of some of your teachers to publicly thank those who taught them in the past.

We Love R Teachers

Sample Invitation to Teacher Recognition Event

OFFICIAL NOTIFICATION

You have definitely won one of the following five prizes:

PRIZE #1—a red Porsche

PRIZE #2—a two-week vacation for two to Tahiti

PRIZE #3—a Mitsubishi Giant Screen TV

PRIZE #4—a mountain chalet at Lake Arrowhead

PRIZE #5—a delicious serving of pie and ice cream

To discover which prize you have won, call (leader) at (phone number) within three days of receiving this notice. Don't be like Mrs. Edna Forbush of Webfoot, Oregon, who missed out on two glamorous weeks in Tahiti with her husband, Gurn. Imagine how Fitch Abercrombie of Upper Downer, Wyoming feels about failing to claim his powerful new Porsche.

You have definitely won one of the above prizes. All it takes is a phone call and that mountain chalet could be yours!

P.S. While you're making the phone call, please let us know the kind of pie you and your spouse or guest would prefer at the Pie Social and Sunday School Teacher Celebration on (day and date) at (time) P.M. (location).

Remember, the number to call is (phone number) to claim your prize.

Teacher Awards

PP.123-129 Reproducible

Complete award certificates to be given at the end of the teaching term, at a dedication service or at a teacher recognition event. Enlist one or more students (and parents) from each teacher's class to hand out the certificates. Photocopy the certificates in this chapter onto heavy, colored paper. They can also be colored with felt pens, glitter pens, etc.

Teacher Contracts/ Job Descriptions

If a job is important enough to ask someone to do it, it is important enough to provide a written definition of what the job entails. A contract is valuable in clarifying everyone's expectations while communicating a sense that the job is significant.

A good contract is marked by several important characteristics:

1. Define starting and ending dates.

Even if the expectation is that a person will continue to serve longer than the ending date, it is wise to have a clearly understood point at which leaders will talk personally with a teacher about continuing, or possibly moving to another area of ministry.

2. Clearly state objectives of the role.

Why should a person give time and energy to this job? How will doing this ministry contribute to the overall mission of the church?

3. List the specific tasks expected.

What are the basic things a person should do in order to succeed in this ministry task? Include explanatory statements of why each action is important and how it will benefit the teacher by helping him or her succeed. (For example, "It is important to get each session off to a good start. Allow opportunity for friendly, informal conversations as children arrive. In order to allow for this relaxed beginning teachers need to be in their rooms, ready to welcome and guide children at least 15 minutes before the announced starting time of the session.")

4. Specify support the person will receive.

What will the church provide to assist the teacher in successful ministry? What resources, materials, supplies, training and personnel assistance is available?

The Christian Education Commitment to Sunday School Teachers

Acting as representatives for the Christian Education Committee, we commit to the following responsibilities:

✦ Be available to provide loving support, encouragement and counsel.

✦ Provide regularly scheduled opportunities for teacher growth: fellowship, training and coordinated planning.

✦ Review, recommend and provide curriculum resources.

✦ Recruit teachers and other staff as needed.

✦ Provide suitable supplies, environment and equipment.

✦ Plan special events to stimulate interest in the Sunday School.

✦ Encourage communication between teachers, parents and church leaders.

_____
Christian Education Representative

_____
Sunday School Coordinator

Sample Contract

SUNDAY SCHOOL CONTRACT

I, _____ , because I feel called by God, commit to the following guidelines as a Sunday School teacher for the period of _____ to _____.
This commitment is reviewable and renewable.

As a Sunday School teacher, I will

✦ Serve on the teaching team for the _____ class/department.

As a Sunday School teacher, I am committed to

Our Lord

✦ I have a personal relationship with Jesus Christ which I desire to model for children.

✦ I enjoy studying God's Word regularly and desire to grow in my faith and commitment to Him (through personal study, adult classes or home Bible study groups).

Our Church

✦ I worship regularly with our church family.

✦ I support the doctrinal statement and leadership of our church.

My Students

✦ I enjoy children and desire for them to know of God's love and concern for their lives.

✦ I will take the necessary time to prepare my lessons during the week, incorporating my own God-given gifts into each lesson.

✦ I will care for my students individually (through prayer, telephone calls, birthday cards, etc.).

✦ I will be faithful in attendance, arriving at least 15 minutes before the session begins. If I must be absent, I will contact an approved substitute and alert the Sunday School Coordinator.

✦ I will follow up with mailings or visits to absentee class members.

✦ I will participate in at least one training event during the year to improve my teaching skills.

My Teaching Team

✦ I will communicate regularly with my team teachers.

✦ I will participate in scheduled teachers' meetings.

✦ I will care for and return all equipment and curriculum provided.

✦ I will express my needs as a teacher to the Christian Education Committee.

_____
Teacher

Teacher Training

PP.131-133 Reproducible

Effective teacher training is an essential ingredient in any church which seeks to build a quality ministry to children. This training must be provided as an ongoing process for the following reasons:

♦ New, inexperienced staff deserve immediate assistance in developing the skills necessary to succeed.

♦ All staff members need repeated exposures to essential goals and procedures in order to develop momentum and consistency.

♦ Even experienced teachers need opportunities to be refreshed and to evaluate their efforts. Otherwise they quickly become stagnant.

♦ Each Sunday brings new children and/or new challenges, requiring teachers who are being helped to grow in their ministry.

Effective teacher training is marked by four major characteristics:

1. It focuses on the age level being taught

While principles of learning are essentially the same for all age-groups, teachers need specific applications of these principles for their own age division. Hold departmental or divisional training sessions, or divide the large group into age-level groups when responding to a general presentation.

2. It is practical

The focus of training should always be on specific things the teachers can implement in their next session.

3. It relates to the curriculum

Teachers should be shown how their curriculum resources help them continue to implement a new procedure or concept.

4. It is experiential

Unless a teacher tries a new skill or method, he or she may not feel confident enough to use it in class.

Provide training for your teachers in these three major formats:

1. Special Training Events

Every year provide two or more training workshops or seminars for your teachers. You may take them to a local, regional or denominational convention or seminar. You may cooperate with one or more other churches in your area. Or, you may plan and conduct the event just for your own people.

An ongoing challenge with such events is that the people who need them the most are the least likely to attend. For that reason, give major attention to how you promote the event, being sure to present it as a benefit, not an obligation. Call it something beside "Teacher Training Meeting." Consider names like "Blueprint for Teachers," "Teacher Fitness Day," or "World's Finest Teachers Conference"—that last one had better be good! (See pages 131-133 in this chapter for sample training event headlines to use in publicizing your training events.)

2. Individual Training and Development

Whether people attend the planned training events or not, whether they serve on a regular,

continuing basis or just a month (or week) at a time, there are many informal opportunities to assist them in doing a better job.

♦ Let them observe an experienced teacher in action.

♦ Provide articles, videos, books to use at home. (See "Teacher Training Resources" article on pages 247 and 248.)

♦ Observe the person in action, then affirm every strong point (perhaps suggesting one or two ways to improve).

♦ Make a point to see or telephone the person to share specific information, such as to (a) explain the layout and components of the curriculum resources; (b) discuss specific children who may need special attention.

3. Regular Teachers' Meetings

Every time teachers get together, include a training feature. Plan a calendar of meetings (weekly, monthly, or quarterly) to help teachers and leaders arrange their schedules. On the calendar list the specific topics you will deal with at each meeting throughout the year.

Teachers' Meetings

PP.135-141 Reproducible

It is important for teachers to meet together because:

♦ They need spiritual, emotional and practical support from each other (see Ecclesiastes 4:9-12).

♦ They will increase their effectiveness and satisfaction as they develop shared goals and strategies.

- They will improve their teaching skills as they share problems and ideas.
- They will better meet the needs of children as they share insights and concerns.

Five basic things should happen when teachers meet together (Items four and five can be done when two or more teachers teach the same or similar lesson content.):

1. Ministry to Each Other

- Begin by sharing what is going on in each other's lives. If people do not know each other well, refreshments, name tags and an ice-breaker activity may be needed to encourage communication. (See pages 33-35 for name tag ideas. See pages 139-141 in this chapter for ice-breaker ideas.)
- Include Bible study of one class' lesson for the next Sunday, discussing how the passage relates to current life situations.
- Pray for one another, for each other's families and for the children and their families as well.

2. Teacher Skill Improvement

Focus on one specific topic at each meeting. Involve teachers in activities and discussion to help them improve that one aspect of teaching.

3. Enthusiasm Builder

Encourage teachers to use one or more of the interest-building ideas suggested in chapter 2.

- Before the teachers' meeting select one or more ideas to present and make copies of the reproducible art.
- At the meeting explain the value and purpose of the interest builder and lead teachers in planning how to implement the idea. Distribute copies of the appropriate art.

4. Content Preview

Survey the Bible content and learning aims of the coming lesson or lessons. Choose and practice songs which support the learning goals.

5. Lesson Planning

Focus on the next session, planning activities and procedures and listing materials suggested in the teacher's manual.

A good meeting requires:

- advance publicity (church bulletin, postcards, posters at church) stating the reason for getting together;
- personal contacts by a leader to secure commitments to attend;
- provision for child care which does not burden the teachers;
- clearly defined starting and ending time on which people can depend;
- excitement over those who attended, not complaints about those who are absent;
- follow-up by leaders to implement plans, informing any who were not present.

As a Teacher You Are:

- ☐ a. Intelligent
- ☐ b. Thoughtful
- ☐ c. Loving
- ☐ d. Creative

FOLD IN HALF.

THANK-YOU CARDS ✦ CHAPTER FOUR ✦ 115

INSIDE

f. All of the above

Thanks for
everything!

Any Job Worth Doing is Worth Doing Well!

HOME SWEET HOME

FOLD IN HALF.

And that's just what you did!

Thanks,

If you can find your way around in your Bible, thank a Sunday School teacher!

THUMBS UP TO OUR TEACHERS!

SUNDAY SCHOOL TEACHERS AT WORK!

CHILDREN UNDER CONSTRUCTION

TEACHER FEATURE

We Love R Teachers

FOCUS on TEACHERS

Teacher of the Month

VIP TEACHER

Certificate of Merit

This Certificate is Presented to:

_____

in recognition of outstanding teaching at:

_____

Signed _____

ALL-STAR TEACHER

WORLD'S GREATEST SUBSTITUTE

WORLD'S GREATEST

THANK YOU • THANK YOU • THANK YOU • THANK YOU • THANK YOU • THANK YOU

WE CAN'T SAY IT ENOUGH!

Thank you for _____

_____

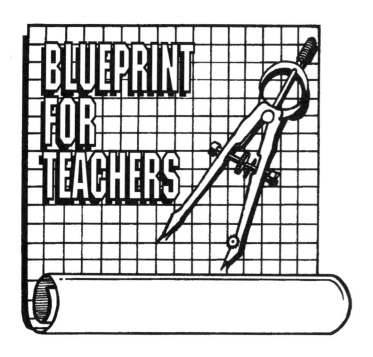

BLUEPRINT FOR TEACHERS

PTO
Parent/Teacher Opportunity

TEACHER FITNESS DAY

When the Teaching Gets Tough, the Teachers Get _Training!_

Teachers don't grow on trees, we grow through TRAINING!

THE ABC'S OF TEACHING SUNDAY SCHOOL

BASIC TRAINING FOR TEACHERS

Top 10 Reasons to come to our Teachers' Meeting

10. Going to a meeting is more fun than doing chores at home.

9. Your significant other will be impressed by your dedication.

8. Your kids may be asleep by the time you come home.

7. Cookies and coffee meet new nutritional guidelines.

6. You might receive the Teacher-of-the-Year award.

5. No offering will be taken.

4. Absentees are always assigned the hardest jobs.

3. You won't have to think of any excuses.

2. It's free.

1. And the number one reason to come to our Teachers' Meeting?

You will enjoy great fellowship and gain terrific teaching tips!

♥

We Train Teachers as if Lives Depended on It!

Get Your Hands on Some Practical Teaching Training

teacher (mod'l) n

1. an example for imitation or emulation.

Did you notice? Someone's following you. That's why another word for teacher could be "model."

To help you be the kind of teacher you want to be, come to our next Teachers' Meeting.

A promise to share helpful teaching ideas.

A promise to encourage your ministry to children.

A promise to start and end on time.

Nothing binds us one to the other like a promise kept. Nothing divides us like a promise broken.
At our teachers' meetings, we believe in keeping our promises.

WORD SCRAMBLE

Unscramble each of these words. You'll find a list of essential teacher materials.

1. OLVE _____

2. PCEEIATN _____

3. TUQESSNOI _____

4. ERANWSS _____

5. MAGES _____

6. GNOSS _____

7. LICPNES _____

8. ISTROSE _____

9. UHMRO _____

10. BBLSEI _____

ANSWERS: 1. LOVE; 2. PATIENCE; 3. QUESTIONS; 4. ANSWERS; 5. GAMES; 6. SONGS; 7. PENCILS; 8. STORIES; 9. HUMOR; 10. BIBLES

If I had to choose...

Circle your answer. Then tell your answer to at least one other person.

A MOVIE
a. musical comedy
b. adventure film
c. love story
d. western

A FOOD
a. frog legs
b. grits
c. escargot
d. venison

A RESTAURANT
a. sushi bar
b. fast-food
c. Chinese
d. Italian

A SPORT
a. baseball
b. couch potato
c. boxing
d. synchronized swimming

I Remember

TELL YOUR ANSWER TO THE FOLLOWING:

1. MY FIRST BIG TRIP
2. MY FAVORITE TV PROGRAM AS A KID
3. MY FIRST JOB
4. MY FIRST KISS
5. MY FAVORITE ROOM
6. MY FAVORITE TEACHER

TEACHER CONCENTRATION

Concentrate on these 13 objects for one minute. At the signal, turn over the page and list the objects from memory. You'll have two minutes.

CHAPTER FIVE

Target New Teachers

"I know you're very busy, and I know the kids can be a pain, and I wish we had someone who could work with you, and I feel bad about asking you to give up going to your adult class, and I know next Sunday is short notice, and maybe after a few months if it doesn't work out we could find someone else to finish out the term—so you probably wouldn't want to try teaching the third graders, would you? No, I didn't suppose you would."

The following chapter is the opposite attitude of that opening paragraph. The next few pages are filled with intriguing, eye-catching—even fun—recruiting plans which attract potential teachers. In approaching people about getting involved in teaching children, you need to help them catch a vision of success, to see themselves making a positive impact on children's lives. It is important to make the entry point into teaching challenging, but achievable—and well worth the doing!

Recruiting Guidelines

Before jumping into the wealth of ideas in this chapter, consider these essential steps in effective recruiting of staff.

1. Keep all the leaders of your Sunday School and other children's ministries aware of and praying about staffing needs. If recruiting is made the total responsibility of only a few leaders, they often become overworked and discouraged. Also, recruiting efforts tend to be made again and again to the same, limited pool of people recruiters know personally. Let everyone know when there are vacancies.

Ask everyone with any involvement in children's ministry to pray regularly that the right person will be enlisted. Encourage them to suggest people they know who could be considered as possible prospects for a vacancy.

2. Regularly present to the congregation information about the goals, benefits and opportunities for ministry with children. People do not want to make a commitment to an organization or program about which they are unfamiliar. Nor do they get excited about becoming part of a group which always seems to be making desperate appeals for somebody—anybody—to help.

Consistently present your children's Sunday School in a positive light. Communicate what God is accomplishing, what you are trying to achieve, some of the benefits both children and teachers are receiving. Communicate excitement about your ministry.

3. Develop a written job description for each position on your Sunday School staff. People deserve to know what they are being asked to do. (See "Teacher Contracts/ Job Descriptions" sec-tion on pages 104 and 105 in chapter 4.)

4. Continually identify prospects for your staff, keeping in mind the goal of helping people find fulfilling places of ministry. Avoid the trap of only looking for prospects when you face a vacancy. By actively seeking to discover people with the potential for ministry, the focus can be on finding the position which fits the person, rather than trying to squeeze the person into the job.

Consider everyone in your congregation in your discovery efforts. Use the church membership list, new members' classes, adult class rolls, suggestions from adult teachers or leaders, lists of previous teachers, survey forms. Consider parents, singles, seniors, collegians. Get recommendations from present teachers.

Keep in mind that few, if any, of the people in Scripture that God enlisted for service had volunteered. Many worked diligently to try to talk God out of calling them. The starting place for enlisting people is to identify those who care about serving God, who have shown they have the potential to become effective in working for Him.

5. Prayerfully prioritize your prospect list. Of all the people who could possibly be contacted, who should be approached first? Determine any requirements a person must meet in order to be considered—church member? Personal qualities?

Involve responsible leaders in your church in evaluating or approving those to be contacted. Some prospects may need to be eliminated from consideration due to other commitments they have made of which your children's ministry team is unaware.

6. Personally contact the prospects. A personal letter is a good first step, allowing the prospect to consider the matter without the pressure of someone eagerly looking for a response. Follow up the letter with a phone call to make an appointment for a face-to-face meeting when the ministry can be explained and the prospect can ask questions. **NOTE:** If you are enlisting a large number of people, it may not be possible to initially meet individually with every prospect. An alternative is to schedule one or more dessert meetings to which prospects are invited. Then schedule individual interviews to discuss the prospect's background and qualifications for teaching children. Follow your church's guidelines for volunteer recruitment.

7. Provide opportunities for prospects to observe the ministry in action before making a final decision. Be sure the teacher(s) being observed are doing a capable job. Provide suggestions of what the prospect can look for while observing, and arrange for someone to talk with the prospect about what was seen.

8. Encourage the prospect to take time to prayerfully consider this invitation and to discuss it with family members before making a decision. Usually, one week after observing a class is adequate.

9. Make a follow-up contact with the prospect for an answer—and

accept the decision. Avoid arm-twisting. If the answer is no, be gracious in thanking the prospect for having taken the time to explore this ministry.

10. Provide orientation and training to help the new staff member make a good beginning.

Publicity Aids

PP.149-163
Reproducible

Think for a moment about what you would like a prospective teacher to know about teaching children BEFORE he or she is first approached about getting involved. Since most adults recall having once been children themselves, and many of those had at least some experience attending Sunday School as a child, almost everyone has some preconceived ideas of what children's Sunday School is all about. If those preconceptions are negative ones ("Sunday School was boring!" "Mr. Klink was sure an old crab!" "Boy, did we give those teachers a hard time!"), you will be fighting an uphill battle from the start.

The publicity materials in this chapter (bulletin/newsletter announcements, recruiting letters, posters, fliers, banners, etc.) will provide people with some positive information about teaching. These aids help people see the values and benefits of ministry to children, building a receptivity for the time when you approach them about getting involved. Do not expect that running a few of these notices in your bulletin will suddenly move people to eagerly volunteer. (Remember, even the burning bush did not get Moses to enlist.)

Use these publicity aids throughout the year to keep people aware of the value of children's ministry. However, the major benefit of these aids comes when you use them in advance of and during times when you are actively enlisting people to serve. Use them in letters to preselected prospects whom you are seeking to enlist. (See pages 71-75 in chapter 3 and pages 187-189 in chapter 7 for additional bulletin and newsletter inserts which could be used as part of a recruiting program.)

Skits

PP.165-169
Reproducible

Short skits are an effective way to evoke for the congregation or adult Sunday School classes the value of children's ministry and the opportunities for service. A skit grabs more attention than a simple verbal announcement. Also, if it is well done, a skit conveys a sense that the people who work with children are innovative and have a good time in what they do. (See pages 193-195 in chapter 7 for additional skits.)

The skits in this chapter can be done with puppets, with live actors, or with a combination.

Gimmicks

The ideas in this category range from attention-getters that create interest and excitement to informative communication devices. In all cases, the intent is to both raise awareness of the value of ministry with children and to motivate preselected people to consider getting personally involved.

1. Balloons

Pick a Sunday to begin recruiting teachers. Attach a helium-filled balloon to a personal letter for each person being asked to consider teaching Sunday School. Distribute the balloons and letters either as people arrive at church, or as the service is dismissed. Have a few extras ready to give to people who want to know why they're not being given a balloon. Simply explain, "These are for people who are being asked to prayerfully consider teaching children in Sunday School. We'd love for you to start praying about that, too." Hand-deliver the balloons to the homes of prospects who are missed. **NOTE:** Be sure you clear this "gimmick" with your pastor. An auditorium adorned with numerous balloons is certainly festive and attention-getting, but the pastor deserves to be let in on this in advance. Be sure to attach long ribbons to balloons so they float above eye level. **OPTION:** Enlist children to do the actual giving out of the balloons.

2. Letter from a Child

Have every child in Sunday School write a letter asking for a teacher (e.g., "I need you to be my teacher because...," or "Please be my teacher! I need to learn...."). Enclose one or more children's letters with each recruiting letter.

3. Cookies

Give each prospect a heart-shaped cookie with a note about sharing love through teaching.

4. Flower/Seeds/Seedling

Give each prospect a flower, a seed packet, or a seedling along with a letter about helping children to grow.

5. Candle

Give each prospect a small votive candle glued to a poster board shape with a Bible verse lettered by a child: "You are the light of the world" (Matthew 5:14). Accompany it with a letter inviting the person to help spread God's light in the lives of children.

6. Dedication/ Baptism/ Confirmation

Whenever a child is dedicated, baptized or confirmed, include reminders of the responsibility and opportunity that belongs to each person in the church family to provide nurture for the youngest members.

- Include a brief pastoral exhortation to the congregation as well as to the parents.
- Invite all those currently involved in teaching children to stand during the prayer to affirm their commitment to loving children.
- Have ready at such events an easy device for people to request further information: a coupon or flier in the bulletin, a card in the pew rack, etc.

7. Awards/Bibles

Most churches at some time during the year make some type of award presentation to some of their children. It may be the presentation of a Bible, or recognition for some achievement in Bible memory, attendance or

other accomplishment. At such moments, include an invitation for people to get involved in support of children's ministry. For example, when giving out Bibles, have the children stand at the front for a moment after receiving them. Ask the congregation, "Have we fulfilled our obligation to these children by giving them a copy of God's Word? Or does God also expect us to help them learn to use it, to understand it, to apply it to their lives? Who will teach these children the riches that this Book contains? Will you?" Have ready an easy device for people to request further information about teaching.

8. Child Ushers

When you want to distribute to the total congregation information about getting involved in children's ministries, enlist children to hand it out. You may have them:

- accompany the adult ushers when the offering is being received (the adult passes the plate, the child passes the fliers);
- stand at the doors at the beginning or end of a service to give each person a copy.

9. Children's Ministries Booth

Set up a children's ministries booth in a heavily trafficked area. Display art or other Bible learning projects done by children. Include a VCR showing classroom action. Have several children give out recruiting fliers. Have several sign-up sheets (on clipboards or posters mounted on the wall) on which people can indicate an interest in specific ministries. Give certain people an invitation to come to the booth on Sunday. The booth can be set up for children's ministry only, or as part of a ministry fair with other church ministries.

Sample Recruiting Letters

Dear (name):

Do you remember how startled Jesus' closest friends were the night He wrapped a towel around His waist and washed their feet—a job that none of them wanted to take on? Do you remember what He said to explain His actions to them—and to us?

"You call me Teacher and Lord, and it is right that you do so because that is what I am. I, your Lord and Teacher, have just washed your feet. You, then, should wash one another's feet. I have set an example for you, so that you will do just what I have done for you" (see John 13:13-15).

The children of (church name) have a need for adults like you to guide and teach them about faith in God. That's right—adults just like you. Adults who care, adults who seek to know and follow God in today's world.

We have many opportunities for you to "test the water," to be part of a team that works together providing support and encouragement for each other. We provide outstanding curriculum resources which carefully present effective learning experiences for both children and teachers to enjoy.

Recognizing that God is the giver of many different gifts, we are asking you to prayerfully consider God's call to you. During the next week, someone from the children's ministries team will call to talk with you about our areas of opportunity and to answer any questions you may have. Or, you can beat us to the punch by calling any of us who have signed below.

Because we are deeply concerned about the children of our church and our community, and because we care that you find a place of ministry which enriches your life, we will be praying that God will guide you as you consider this invitation to serve.

Sincerely,

(names, titles, phone numbers)

Dear (name):

On a recent Sunday morning, has your attention been drawn a little closer to the ground than usual—and focused for a few moments on one of the children in (church name)'s family? Sometimes it's the noise that our ear picks up—or the quick movement that catches the eye—but there is something about those younger people that is sometimes hard to ignore, even when we might like to do so!

The people around Jesus did their best to ignore children:
◆ They tried to shoo them away from disturbing an important grown-up discussion.
◆ They scoffed at the idea that a boy's lunch could be of any value to a crowd of hungry adults.
◆ They complained about children praising Jesus in the Temple.

Jesus felt those grown-ups should have known better, so He rebuked them. One time He set a child in the middle of the crowd to teach His followers what God's kingdom is really like. God's kingdom—and our church—needs children, even noisy, active children. We need children not just to prepare for the future, but as constant reminders of the value God places on every human life. That's right—children teach us even as we teach them.

On behalf of our children's ministries team, I would like to invite you to participate in a ministry to children during the next year. The positive qualities you demonstrate in the life of our church are the characteristics our children need to see in the adults who teach them, laugh with them, listen to them, and become their models of the Christian life.

(Add a summary of children's ministry opportunities, and your plan to follow up on this letter.)

Sincerely,

(names, titles, phone numbers)

Sample Recruiting Letters

LETTER FOR PALM SUNDAY

Dear (name):

Most people don't associate balloons with Palm Sunday. But if Jesus were to have made His entry into Jerusalem this spring, people in the crowds probably would release colorful balloons to express their joy.

That is why we chose this balloon to present to you—we want it to represent the joy of sharing the love of Jesus with children.

We sense the same joy today as we invite you to consider becoming involved in our Sunday School's ministry to children during the next year.

Sincerely,

(names, titles, phone numbers)

MEMO

TO:
(name of prospect)

SUBJECT:
Jake, Renee, Kim, John, Megan, Bobby, Natalie, Samantha, Morgan, Brandon, Kristi, Hannah, Tricia, Darren, Chantel, Jon, Michael, Ryan, Ashley, Jason, Carrell, Matthew, Danny, Jerith, Brian, Miles, Robbie, Michelle, Christopher, Roxie, Frank, Timmy, Amy, Katie, Hayley, Corrie, Rachel, Joey, Keith, Sarah, Ayla, Lindsay, Jennie.

These are just some of the children entrusted to our care in the (name of church) family. Each one is learning and growing in God's love because people care. We are asking you to consider being part of a team which shares Jesus' love with a group of these in the Sunday School hour at (time) during the coming year.

Sincerely,

(leader's name and title)

A Sample Letter Enlisting Short-Term Personnel

Dear Family:

During the past year-and-a-half, much of the loving care for young children in the (name of program) has been provided by families with Middle School and High School students like yours. Each month, as a family has taken a turn in working together in ministry, it has been evident that:

✦ The little ones really like to play with your teenagers.

✦ The children also feel secure with an experienced mom and/or dad.

✦ Their security is helped by being with the same family several weeks in a row.

✦ Both the children and their parents, as well as the teenagers and their parents, enjoy getting to know members of our friendly, extended church family.

The purpose of this letter is to encourage your family to pick a month during the next six months as a family ministry project, caring for little ones in this important program.

You and your teenager(s) can help those with young children, demonstrating the high priority which families have in the life of our church. Please talk together about this opportunity to minister as a family. Then call (phone number) or return the enclosed form indicating your preference of month. Even if you will not be able to participate in this ministry, it will be very helpful if you return the form. This will avoid our assuming you mislaid the letter and bugging you with unnecessary phone calls.

Sincerely,

(leader's name and title)

A Sample Response Form

The _____ **Family**

✦ would love

✦ would like

✦ is willing

✦ has been persuaded

✦ may be persuaded
   (bribery helps)

✦ will not be able
   (so please don't call)

✦ will not be able
   (but we like phone calls)

to help in (name of program) during the month of (please mark three in order of preference)

✦ September

✦ October

✦ November

✦ December

✦ January

✦ February

Signed by each of us, signifying we're of mostly sound mind.

Date: _____

Or, call (leader) at (phone number) right away to beat everyone else to the month you really want.

Everybody talks about "kids these days." Now you can do something about it...

Right now, you can join others who are committed to communicating God's Word to children.
We need your support for our Sunday School.

Plant a seed. Grow a tree.
Teach a child. Grow a life.

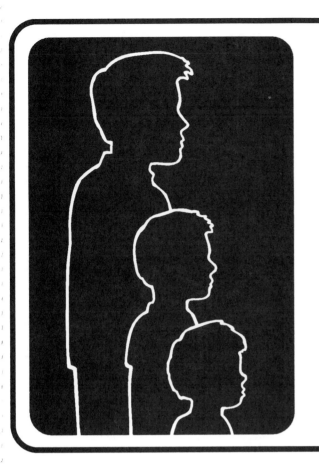

What you teach them now will teach them forever.

Become a part of our teaching team. Your efforts will have a lifetime effect.

Jesus said "Feed my lambs," not "baby-sit" them.

Kids in our church depend on you. They need to know that someone cares. And what better way to show how much you care than as a Sunday School teacher.

SIDE BY SIDE

COME ALONG AND JOIN
OUR TEAM OF SUNDAY
SCHOOL TEACHERS!

"And He took the children in His arms, put
His hands on them, and blessed them."
Mark 10:16

Will you help Jesus touch another child?

WHAT CAN A PERSON DO THAT:

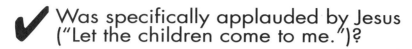

✔ Was specifically applauded by Jesus ("Let the children come to me.")?

✔ Makes a positive difference over a full life span as well as for eternity?

✔ Touches not just an individual, but a whole family?

✔ Nurtures you more than it does the one you help?

✔ Helps you stay young at heart?

YOU CAN BECOME A PART OF OUR SUNDAY SCHOOL TEACHING TEAM!

WE OWE OUR KIDS AN EXPLANATION.

So what's a Christian anyway?

Sunday School helps kids learn the basics of becoming a Christian and living as God's child.

We need you to join our team of Sunday School teachers.

When we're dealing with something as important as the faith of our kids, we owe them that much.

Did You Know?

Did you know that television absorbs more than 20 hours of the average child's week? Are you aware that school involves a child for more than 30 hours per week, plus another 3 to 7 hours of homework? How about Little League which often requires 5 or more hours per week? Or music lessons which expect 2 to 4 hours per week? Then there's the church. It averages less than 1 hour per week of effective personal and spiritual guidance.

Our Sunday School fills a vital need in the lives of children — and every Sunday counts. You can be one of the adults who will grow through serving, loving and teaching a small group of children. You can experience the deep satisfaction of knowing you have influenced a life for Jesus Christ.

A child needs you to be the special person in his or her life. Our church needs you to teach Sunday School.

Some people come into our lives and go quickly.

Some stay awhile and leave footprints in our hearts,

and we are never, ever the same!

Love a Child. Touch the Future.

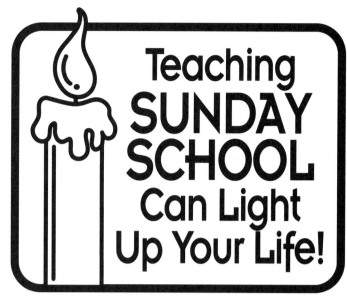

Teaching **SUNDAY SCHOOL** Can Light Up Your Life!

ADMIT ONE

• • • **RESERVED FOR YOU** • • •

PrimeTime For Kids

a unique and exciting opportunity to share Jesus' love with children.

"Teach a child to choose the right path, and when he is older he will remain upon it."

Proverbs 22:6

Hands Across the Years

You Can Bridge the Gap

We Like Your Smile!

Share It with a Child!

Hide 'n Seek

We're SEEKING a few good people to help kids HIDE God's Word in their hearts.

A Series of Brief Encounters— Number 1

Children's Leader: (Enters, carrying clipboard and pen. Speaks to audience.) Hi, there. I'm sorry I haven't really got time to talk now. I've got several people I need to see. (Starts to continue on, then turns back to audience.) I need to see them about getting involved in our children's ministry. Oh, here comes one of the people on my list now.

Mr. Goodsport: (Enters carrying golf clubs, tennis racket, fishing pole, etc. He's singing, perhaps off-key, but enthusiastically.) Hi ho, hi ho, the weekend's here you know. There's golf and tennis and fishing and fun hi ho, hi ho, hi....

Leader: Excuse me, Mr. Goodsport. I'm glad I ran into you. I've been wanting to talk to you about that letter you received from our children's ministry team.

Mr. Goodsport: Letter? Letter? Oh, letter!... Later. I'm on my way to a weekend full of activity. Can you catch me some other time? (Continues on his way, still singing.) Hi ho, hi ho....

Leader: But I wanted to talk to you about the children.

Mr. Goodsport: (Stops, turns back to Leader.) The children? Oh, yes, the children. I'm sorry, but expecting me to be in church every Sunday to baby-sit some children is just out of the question. It's too bad Sunday comes on a weekend. Oops, gotta run. It's later than I thought. (Exits, singing.) Hi ho, hi ho....

Leader: But Mr. Goodsport....(To audience.) He was in such a hurry, I didn't have time to tell him we have a regular substitute for that class. So, on the occasional weekend when a teacher needs to be gone, the substitute can step in. Maybe I can catch up with him on the eighteenth green....(Exits.)

Pastor/Other Leader: I hope (s)he does catch up with Mr. Goodsport. He's filled his life so full of activity, he hasn't left room for ministry. I trust none of you will let this next year slip by without finding the deep satisfaction of serving God and others— perhaps by teaching children.

A Series of Brief Encounters— Number 2

Children's Leader: (Enters, looking at clipboard, making marks with pen, talking to self.) Who haven't I talked to yet about our children's ministry? Saw him. Found her. Saw her. Found him. Here's one! (Looks up.) And here she comes!

Mrs. Past Tense: (Enters, waves.) There you are. I've been looking all over for you.

Leader: What a coincidence—I was looking for you.

Mrs. Past Tense: Thank you for thinking of me with that lovely letter about the children.

Leader: That's why I was looking for you, to find a time when I could share with you some of the exciting things happening with children in our church.

Mrs. Past Tense: Oh, that would be lovely. But, of course, you know I did my turn with Sunday School when my children were young. I'll never forget those years. But now...

Both in unison: ...it's someone else's turn.

Mrs. Past Tense: I'm so glad you agree with me. It's so good of you to put up with those noisy, wiggly kids. I'm so glad I don't have that responsibility any more. (Waves as she exits.) Keep up the good work!

Leader: (To audience, with a touch of sarcasm). Just a minute. I want to write those down. (Slowly while writing.) "It's someone else's turn." (Looks up.) Does the Bible say anything about taking turns with ministry? (Writes again.) "I don't have that re-spon-si-bility an-y more." (Looks up again.) I'll bet she thinks ministry is some type of quota system. Once you've done a good deed, you're exempt!

Mrs. Past Tense: (Returns and interrupts.) Oh, good! You're still here! I was just remembering how good it felt to see a child's eyes light up...

Leader: (Interrupts.) Oh good! I wanted to tell you about a brand new teacher who would love to have a partner with your skills and experience. (They exit together as leader continues explaining.) You'd not only be loving and teaching some wonderful children, you'd be helping us develop a whole new generation of teachers....

Pastor/Other Leader: Who really is responsible for the children of our church and our community? Mrs. Past Tense assumed she was free to walk on by. Maybe she—and all of us—need the message of Proverbs 3:27: "Do not withhold good from those who deserve it, when it is in your power to act."

A Series of Brief Encounters—Number 3

Children's Leader: (Enters carrying clipboard and pen. Speaks to audience.) There's just one person left on my list. Some really great people have accepted the challenge to be part of the Children's Ministry Team. But I haven't been able to find Mr. Vert. Has anyone seen Mr. N. Vert around?

Member: (From back row of audience.) He's back here!

Leader: Back there? Oh, I see him. Mr. Vert! Hi!

Mr Vert: (Gets up from back row, comes forward shyly, hands in pockets or clasped in front.) Well, I've sort of been keeping a low profile.

Leader: Why is that?

Mr. Vert: Ever since I got that letter from the children's ministry team, I've been avoiding all of you.

Leader: Avoiding us?

Mr. Vert: I hoped if you didn't see me around, you'd sort of forget you sent me the letter and then I wouldn't have to invent an excuse not to help out with the children's programs.

Leader: Invent an excuse?

Mr. Vert: (Looks around.) Is there an echo in here?

Leader: (Also looks around.) An echo in here? (Turns to Mr. Vert.) You don't have to invent excuses. We're not trying to twist anyone's arm. We sent you that letter because we feel you have a lot to offer our children.

Mr. Vert: Oh, I'm sure there are many people who could do much better than I could. I'm not really the type for teaching kids.

Leader: I'm not sure there is a "type" for teaching kids. But I do know that someone as friendly and caring and thoughtful as you are is someone who can benefit children.

Mr. Vert: Do you think so? But I've never taught before. I've never done ANYTHING like that before.

Leader: Would you be willing to visit a class and see what goes on—to help you get an idea of what you could do to make a difference for some children?

Mr. Vert: Make a difference? Me? Do you really think I could make a difference?

Leader: (Starts to exit along with Mr. Vert.) I'm sure you could make a big difference. Which of the next three Sundays would be the best time for you to observe a class in action? (Exit.)

Pastor/Other Leader: You may not be as shy as Mr. N. Vert, but you may never have had the exciting privilege of making a real difference in someone's life, either. Our children's ministry team is looking for some friendly, loving, thoughtful people who want to make a positive difference. (Explain how to express an interest in children's ministry.)

CHAPTER SIX

Communicate to Church Leaders

Many churches tend to view the Sunday School—especially children's Sunday School—as though it were an optional appendage, somehow attached to the church, but not really a part of the church's central mission. As a result, churches may give lip service to the importance of reaching and teaching children ("The children of today are the church of tomorrow!"), but, except for those who have children in the program, relatively few people feel drawn to be directly involved.

Some typical comments by children's Sunday School leaders illustrate this all-too-common fact of church life:

"Our pastor never showed any interest in the nursery until his first grandchild was born. Suddenly, he was asking all kinds of questions about our staff, our policies, our cleaning procedures—everything!"

"You could have knocked me over with a feather when our adult leadership scheduled and set up a Sunday luncheon in one of our children's classrooms—and never thought to check with us. It simply never occurred to them that our children needed that space."

"Actually I kind of like being able to pretty well run the program with little or no interference from the board or church staff. As long as we don't make too much noise or break anything, everyone's happy to leave us alone."

"Why is it that the few times I have asked to present a need to the church board, I've felt like I was interrupting their 'real' business? They were polite, but they seemed so...condescending. Do the youth or music or adult leaders feel the same way when they ask for help?"

Churches with strong Sunday Schools have church leaders who understand both the need and the effort necessary to effectively minister to children and their families. Such understanding does not happen by accident. This chapter contains useful tips and ideas for keeping church leaders informed of the mission of the Sunday School so that they can provide positive support for the total ministry of the church.

Communication Tips

Consider these basic guidelines for communicating the important issues of your children's ministries to church leaders and other staff members.

1. Identify the key leaders in your church whose counsel and support are most crucial for your children's ministry. It may be the senior pastor, a church board member, the education committee, another staff member, etc. Which leaders already have a good understanding of the Sunday School? Which ones need to be made more aware of your goals, challenges and achievements?

2. Focus on the positive aspects of your ministry. Identify the key goals and achievements you want to share with other leaders.

✦ What is the Sunday School doing to help the church reach its goals?

✦ What specific efforts are being planned?

✦ What good things have happened recently?

✦ Who are the people who are serving faithfully?

Before mentioning a problem to anyone, always be sure you have laid a solid foundation of favorable comments. No matter if your problems seem overwhelmingly greater than your resources, start with whatever pluses you have before addressing the minuses.

3. Plan a variety of ways and times to bring up matters of concern with leaders. This includes, but goes beyond, regular meetings or those which you might schedule to deal with specific issues.

✦ When might you expect to "run into" this person for a brief moment? (At the water cooler? In the hallway or lobby or parking lot after a church service? On the tennis court?)

✦ What reason could you have for dropping a short note in the mail? (To share a humorous or

171

poignant incident from last Sunday? To offer congratulations for an achievement that person made in his or her area of ministry? To thank the person for a helpful act?)

✦ How about leaving a phone message with a secretary or on an answering machine?

✦ Try clipping a cartoon or article about children from a newspaper or magazine and leaving it on the person's desk.

✦ When could you publicly express appreciation for a person's support?

✦ If you do not regularly attend staff or board meetings, occasionally ask to be included. Make a report about children's ministries.

4. Be ready to take advantage of any natural opportunities to communicate with staff/board while doing something else. For example, at a meeting with a full agenda, simply distribute something of interest from the children's area—samples of art or written Bible Learning Activities from a class or department, comments of interest from teachers, children or parents, a short article about teaching children, etc. (See pages 93-99 in chapter 3 for articles.)

5. When making a presentation in a meeting, plan how you will capture interest and communicate one or more of the positive issues you want to emphasize. For example, show a short video of children singing or acting out a Bible story, play an audiotape of interviews with children, show an overhead transparency featuring information on one of your teachers who deserves recognition, give everyone a chocolate kiss to express thanks for previous support, etc.

6. Look for ways to expose leaders to what is going on in your children's ministry. Create reasons to bring them into the classrooms, meeting children and seeing the teachers in action. A firsthand visit often has far more impact than any presentation you can make. Invite church leaders to be prayer partners for specific Sunday School teachers. (See pages 185 and 186 in chapter 7 for ways to enlist prayer partners.)

7. Lead the children's staff in identifying ways children can provide a service for some other ministry of the church. Some ideas include:

✦ A class works together to pick up papers and/or pull weeds around the church campus.

✦ Children's classes send pictures and letters to missionaries supported by the church and/or to shut-in church members.

✦ A class works together to pick up discarded bulletins and to straighten out hymn books and/or pew Bibles immediately after the worship service.

✦ A class volunteers to assist the ushers/greeters in distributing bulletins and/or receiving the offering.

✦ A class prepares a song, skit or puppet story to present to an adult class.

✦ Children commit to pray for a special need or event.

✦ Children take on a giving project to help another area of ministry.

Cartoons

Reproduce these cartoons and use them in a variety of ways:

✦ Hand out a cartoon at a staff or board meeting before presenting a children's ministry report.

✦ Attach a cartoon to a list of current teachers which will be distributed to church leaders.

✦ Enclose a cartoon with a personal thank-you note to your pastor or other church leader expressing appreciation for his or her efforts on behalf of the children in your church.

Meet the Pastor Day

Invite the pastor or other member of the church staff (along with a different church board member) to visit children's classes or departments. Ask the guests to stay 10-15 minutes, with part of the time given to informal observation and interaction as children are involved in activities. Some of the time may also include enjoying a special snack together, letting children show and explain some of the things they do, and teachers or children interviewing the guests. (Sample questions: What is your job at our church? What is your favorite thing to do at church? At home? What did you like to do when you were our age? How did you learn to love Jesus?) The specifics of what happens will depend on the age-group.

Awards Presentations

Ask a pastor or other leader to present awards occasionally when a class has learned a certain number of Bible verses, brought a specified number of visitors, completed a service project or other class achievement. The presentation could be made in the classroom or as part of the worship service.

Thank-you/ Recognition Letters

P.179 Reproducible

To build relationships between children and church leaders, ask children to write letters to the pastor or other leaders. The letters could mark a birthday or anniversary, expressing thanks for the person's leadership. Or they could be sent after the person has made a specific contribution to the community, the church and/or the children. You may have each child write an individual card or letter, have them work together to compose a single letter, and/or have them sign and decorate one document from their class or from all children in the church. (See pages 109-117 in chapter 4 for thank-you cards.)

Pastor's Talent Time

If your pastor or other leader has a particular talent (musical instrument, singing, or interesting hobby) ask him or her to share it briefly with the children. For example, a pastor who enjoys gardening could bring some potted plants and a collection of tools. Someone who enjoys cycling could show some safety equipment. Someone with musical talent can sing or play several of the children's current songs. Someone with dramatic ability could read a poem or present a monologue.

Worship Preparation

Periodically schedule the pastor or other leader involved in the worship service to visit older children's classes for the last five minutes of Sunday School. This leader can introduce the children to some feature of the morning worship service. This might involve explaining the words of a hymn the congregation will sing, assigning the children to listen for a specific piece of information during the sermon, or to describe the work of the ushers. As a result of this visit, the children will feel more a part of the service which follows—and the adult leader will be more aware of the presence of children and their need to understand what goes on in the worship service.

Getting the Family to Church: The Sunday Morning Marathon

Don't Forget: Reach Down and Touch Someone.

The Challenge of Capturing Parents' Attention.

(Children sign names in blank spaces.)

HAPPY BIRTHDAY, PASTOR!

(Children sign names in blank spaces.)

CHAPTER SEVEN

Connect with Your Congregation

"I had no idea this church was doing so much to reach children!"

"You have a class for one-year-olds? What do you teach them? Advanced Drooling?"

"Excuse me. My grandson is visiting from out of town. Do you have any idea where fourth graders should go?"

"Why don't we schedule it (concert, guest speaker, film, missionary presentation, congregational meeting, etc.) during the Sunday School hour? I'm sure the kids—and teachers—would like an excuse to get out of class."

"Why are we spending all that money on kids? Kids today are spoiled. Seems like a big waste to me."

"If space is a problem, why don't we just put all the kids together in the fellowship hall? We can get a few high schoolers to baby-sit them—maybe they could show videos?"

Believe it or not, all of the above statements were made by long-term, active church members—in some cases, people with major leadership responsibilities. Very few people in any church tend to have a good understanding of every area of the church's ministry. There are always people in the congregation who know little or nothing about the Sunday School or other children's programs.

At first blush, this lack of knowledge seems harmless. "What they don't know won't hurt me" is a fairly widespread attitude among children's leaders who tend to roll their eyes and politely keep their mouths sealed whenever such ignorance is revealed. However, when members of the congregation lack knowledge about children's ministry, the results are eventually damaging. A congregation unaware of children's ministry:

✦ is not a fertile source of potential teachers and leaders;
✦ is unlikely to provide the resources needed for quality programs;
✦ tends to select leaders with little or no awareness of children's needs;
✦ gives priority to other endeavors, often without considering the full implications;
✦ gradually drifts towards becoming an older congregation, losing the needed balance of young families.

In addition to the approaches suggested in this chapter to promote a church-wide awareness about Sunday School, many of the ideas in earlier chapters also contribute to that end.

Bulletin/ Newsletter Inserts

PP.187-191 Reproducible

Provide your bulletin/newsletter editor with a steady steam of quotes or short articles about Sunday School which can be dropped in as fillers. For example: "We're thankful for the great people who teach in our Sunday School. People like (insert name) make a positive impact every week!" (See pages 189-191 in this chapter for additional quotes.)

Sample Bulletin Insert

If you had been in the 3rd—5th Grade Sunday School class last week, you would have:

✦ Experienced what it is like to be blind by trying to draw a picture while blindfolded or identifying common objects by touch.
✦ Explored the account in John 9 of Jesus healing a man who was born blind.
✦ Learned of some people in our church family who have struggled with various handicaps.
✦ Considered ways to show Christ's love to people with various handicaps.
✦ Laughed, sung, prayed, laughed, studied, talked—and maybe laughed some more.

A dedicated team of teachers (names) works every Sunday morning to show God's love to 3rd, 4th and 5th grade children—and open to them the many riches in God's Word.

Skits

PP.193-196 Reproducible

Skits are very effective ways to communicate, as people will focus attention on the message as they listen to a dialog or get involved in a situation. Skits also allow the use of light humor, which helps to retain interest and stimulate recall of the information. In addition, skits allow you to involve people other than the faithful few who tend to do just about everything. Consider the use of puppets, either for all skit characters, or one or more characters that interact with live people.

Poster Parade

During the worship service or in any adult meeting, at predetermined points in the program (e.g., announcements), one or more children walk across the front of the room carrying large signs that ask and answer questions or make announcements. In most cases, the leader should act surprised, stop talking and simply watch the child proceed across the room. Or, the leader may comment on the announcement as the child is walking, or after the child has exited. For example:

✦ One child carries a poster asking "When is a school better than a school?" A minute or so later another child walks through carrying a poster that says: "When it's a Sunday School!" A short time later a third child enters with a poster announcing: "That's at 9:30 EVERY Sunday morning! Don't miss out!"

✦ Instead of simple signs, have someone who likes to draw make a giant cutout of a popular cartoon character, with a blank conversation balloon. Then fit a series of messages to the balloon, changing them each time the cutout is carried through the building.

✦ Several Sundays before a special children's event, have a child walk through the room carrying a sign that says: "It's coming (date)!!" The next week have the same child carry a sign that says: "It's STILL coming (date)!" The next Sunday the sign reads: "It's almost here!" Just before the child exits, the leader exclaims, "OK, I give up! What is this IT that's almost here?" The child either turns the sign around and reveals another sign with the announcement, or another child enters and carries the sign with the details.

✦ During the time when you are actively recruiting teachers and leaders, have a series of signs announcing your progress. The first week a sign is carried by an older child: "Only (27) positions available for loving and teaching kids like me." A few seconds later, a very small child walks through carrying a sign that says "And me, too!" Each succeeding week, a new sign precedes those two. This one says: "Hooray! (4) more wonderful people have agreed to teach Sunday School!" You may even want to add a sign or signs giving the names of those who have been added to your staff. Every week the numbers on the signs change.

✦ Instead of carrying signs through the worship service or other meetings, have children carry signs up and down the hallways, through the foyer, or other area where adults gather before or after services.

Music

Coordinate with your church music leader to occasionally teach the congregation a song one or more children's department has been singing. Have an adult explain what the children have been studying and how this particular song relates to their Bible learning. Arrange for the children to sing the song through once, and then help lead the congregation in singing along. This is most effective when the song correlates with the emphasis of that worship service.

Demonstration Video

Place a video monitor and recorder in the lobby or hallway. Play it before or after services, showing a children's class in action. Place a sign on top of the monitor, identifying the class, the teachers and the focus of the lesson. Provide a bulletin announcement, encouraging people to view it, explaining where the monitor is placed and what is being shown.

Share a Bible Learning Activity

P.197 Reproducible

1. Encourage teachers to think of ways their classes can share some of their Bible Learning Activities outside of their classrooms. For example:

◆ Display art or writing projects on a wall, bulletin board or portable display panel. Locate the display where it will be seen by the maximum possible number of adults. Add a sign that identifies the class, teachers and students. If you have space for a permanent display, change the display at least once a month. You may assign each class or department a specific month in which to display projects.

◆ Some activities lend themselves to being displayed on a table (e.g., models, books, games, etc.). When making a table display, include a poster which can be mounted on a wall or post behind the display to attract attention from a distance.

◆ Present a rhythmic chant of a Bible verse as a feature in a youth or adult class or the worship service. Or do an antiphonal reading of a Bible passage being studied.

◆ Practice a drama or puppet activity so that it can be presented to a youth or adult group. Or enlist several parents or other adults to video tape the presentation, then show the video to several groups.

◆ Share a snack the children have made with a youth or adult class.

◆ Include samples of art or writing projects (prayers, poems, short stories, etc.) in the church newsletter or bulletin.

2. Communicate with teachers well ahead of time to get activities organized for effective sharing. For example, if a display will be made, teachers need three to four weeks to collect and label a variety of student work.

3. Teachers' involvement in organizing the sharing should be kept to a minimum. This is a great spot for parent or senior citizen help—or to involve people who work with children as a career, but do not want to do so regularly on Sundays.

4. Provide a bulletin announcement which invites the congregation to visit the display. Arrange for teachers and/or children to stand by the display to answer questions and simply be friendly.

Sample Bulletin Announcements

In the (location) today is a display of some of the work our Sunday School children have done in recent weeks. Take a few minutes to look at what they've done and to talk to a teacher about the many ways our children are growing in their understanding of God's love and care.

Take a minute or two this morning to see the Neat, Interesting and Great display in the (location). You will enjoy seeing this recent work by our (age-level) Sunday School Department.

(**Note:** Page 197 in this chapter provides the **LEARNING** clip art.)

Printed/ Verbal Announcements

PP.197-201 Reproducible

Combining two or more communication forms greatly increases the impact of the message. To get extra mileage out of an announcement, build a link between verbal and printed information. Typically, this is done simply by having someone say, "I want to call your attention to the announcement in the bulletin...." Then the written announcement is merely read aloud or rephrased. Consider the following ideas for going beyond that basic approach.

A Sample Series of Bulletin and Pulpit Announcements
Introducing a New Sunday School Emphasis—Prime Time for Kids

A SERIES OF PULPIT ANNOUNCEMENTS

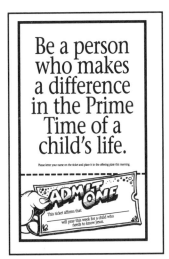

Week 1—Before Welcome/Greeting Time

Plans are now being made for the start of an exciting new emphasis in children's Sunday morning ministry. It will start (date), and we're calling it "Prime Time for Kids" to focus attention on the importance of the childhood years in forming values and understanding. Please look at the ticket printed in your bulletin and the statement below which asks you to pray this week for one child who will benefit from being part of Prime Time for Kids. It may be a child sitting near you now, or one you know from your neighborhood.

During our time of greeting one another, if you're 12 years old or older, make sure you shake hands with at least one person younger than 12 and say, "Prime Time starts (date)!"

Week 2—Before Welcome/Greeting Time

Plans are well underway for the start of an exciting new emphasis in children's ministry. "Prime Time for Kids" will start (date) to focus attention on the importance of the childhood years in forming values and understanding. Please look at the ticket printed in your bulletin and the statement below which asks you to pray this week for a parent whose child can benefit from being part of Prime Time for Kids. It may be a parent sitting near you now, or someone you know from work or your neighborhood.

During our time of greeting one another, if you're 12 years old or older, make sure you shake hands with at least one person younger than 12 and say, "Prime Time starts (date)!"

Week 3—Before the Offering

When you were a child, were you ever the last player chosen for a game? Do you remember what it felt like to learn of a birthday party to which you had not been invited? All of us have memories of times when we felt left out. If there is one place where no child should ever be left out, it's our exciting new Prime Time for Kids. Prime Time starts (date) from 9:30-10:30 every Sunday morning. Take a moment right now and think of a child—in your family, your neighborhood, the child of a friend from work. Then complete the "Prime Time for Kids" ticket and place it in the offering plate this morning.

Week 4—Before the Offering

Prime Time for Kids is the name for our Sunday morning ministry for children. Starting (date), from 9:30-10:30, you can be one of the adults who will grow as part of a team which serves, loves and teaches a small group of children. You can experience the deep satisfaction of knowing you have influenced a life for Jesus Christ. To learn more about how you can minister to a child, complete the "Prime Time for Kids" ticket—and place it in the offering plate this morning.

Open House

P.201 Reproducible

Invite the congregation to an Open House in the children's Sunday School rooms. Enlist parents to provide a different refreshment in each department. As the congregation exits, give each person or family unit a ticket telling which room the recipient is to visit so that the crowd is somewhat evenly distributed. In each classroom prominently display samples of the children's work, along with pictures of the classes in action. (Some groups may show videos, others can have a slide projector running, others may display posters with snapshots.) All teachers and leaders should be given name tags.

Other Presentations

If your church has a children's sermon or "Moment for Children" in worship services, or if adult Sunday School classes are receptive to occasional visits from children, consider ways these opportunities can be used to present various aspects of your children's ministry. A few examples include:

✦ An interview with several children about why they like Sunday School and what they are learning. (A GREAT interview to have the pastor do!)

✦ An interview with a teacher about why he or she invests time in teaching children.

✦ Special music by a child. For example, a child who is taking music lessons could present a song his or her class has been singing.

✦ Make overhead transparencies or slides of children's art or writing and project it. For example, at Christmas letter the words of Christmas carols onto sheets of paper, one line or phrase per page. Have children illustrate each page, then transfer to transparencies. Project these illustrations as the congregation sings the carols.

Memory Booklet

P.203 Reproducible

Ask 10-12 adults in the church to write a brief account of a favorite or humorous Sunday School memory. Or have them write about "A Teacher I Remember." Give simple guidelines to direct their writing:

1. Keep it brief—three to five paragraphs.

2. Be specific—tell about a specific event or person, not just general impressions.

3. Tell it like a story—we want families to read this to their children, and kids love stories!

4. Describe how you felt then—and how you feel now. If you liked or disliked something, let your emotions show.

Add a brief statement on the value of Sunday School for children today. Compile these into a

5x8 1/2-inch (12.5x21.25-cm) booklet and have a child draw the cover design. Or use the reproducible covers in this chapter. Hand out the booklets to the congregation with instructions to read the stories aloud as a family (perhaps one each day at dinner time). Suggest that families talk about each story, telling ways in which Sunday School today is similar or different.

A similar booklet can be done to promote VBS, children's camp or other special event. A booklet on the theme "A Christmas Memory I Treasure" is also a nice addition to the Christmas season.

Prayer Time

Provide information to your pastor or other leader of a specific need or praise report to be included as part of the pastoral prayer in the worship service. Provide similar information to groups or individuals who have committed to pray for needs of the church.

Prayer Reminders

P.205 Reproducible

Distribute small prayer reminders to the congregation. These can be placed in the bulletin, handed out as people leave the worship service, or printed in the newsletter. You may want to print them on index cards that can be attached to the refrigerator or a home bulletin board. List three or four specific items for prayer.

Sample Prayer Requests

Pray for the Children

As you pray:

◆ Mention a specific child by name, that he or she will grow in understanding of God's love.

◆ Ask God to provide our children's teachers with the energy, patience and love they need and desire.

◆ Focus on this coming Sunday morning, asking that each child will be drawn closer to Jesus.

◆ Give thanks for the wonderful people who dedicate their time and energy to teaching and loving children in our Sunday School.

Also print a bulletin announcement on the week the reminders are distributed. For example:

Pray for the Children

Today as you leave the worship service, some of the children and teachers in our Sunday School will be distributing Prayer Reminder cards. These cards suggest ways you can support our children's ministry with your prayers. You may attach your card to your refrigerator, a bulletin board, or place it in your Bible—wherever it will help you remember to pray for our children and their faithful teachers.

Prayer Partners

P.205 Reproducible

Invite members of the congregation (or of adult classes) to commit to be a prayer partner for a specific Sunday School teacher during the coming quarter, semester or year.

To enlist prayer partners:

1. Print a prayer partner registration form in the bulletin or newsletter. Run the "ad" for several weeks.

2. Make announcements in worship services and adult classes inviting people to commit to pray regularly for a specific teacher and class. Suggest several specific needs for which people can pray:

◆ Children whose parents do not attend church. (Don't name them, but people would be interested in knowing how many such children attend your Sunday School.)

◆ Families of teachers.

◆ Continued spiritual growth by teachers.

◆ Classes which need additional teacher help. (You can name these.)

◆ An upcoming Sunday School event.

3. Arrange for several people to share experiences in which they were benefitted by the prayers of someone else.

When prayer partners and teachers have been matched:

1. Schedule a Prayer Partner Sunday on which all the prayer part-

ners visit the classes of the teachers for whom they will be praying.

2. Suggest that prayer partners call teachers to find out prayer requests at least once a month. (Alert teachers to be sensitive to sharing information about personal or family problems of children in their class. It is not necessary for prayer partners to always know the names or details in order to pray for a child's need.)

3. Occasionally, have teachers lead their classes in making and sending to the prayer partners items such as thank-you cards, prayer request lists, and/or samples of special learning activities.

> *Prayer Partner*
> ## MEMO
> MY PARTNER:
> CLASS:
> PRAY FOR:

Here's Some of the Many Little Reasons Our Church Has a Sunday School.

As you come to church each week, it doesn't take long to realize that our church is a family place. You'll see children smiling, laughing and talking as our church family gathers for a special time of learning about God's Word.

You Don't Run Across Durability Like This Every Day.

Since 1780 when the first Sunday School met, millions of people—children and adults—have learned how God's Word truly makes a difference in their lives.

FOUNDED 1780

"Children have more need of models than of critics."

Joseph Joubert

"Our Sunday School— Where Kids Meet Their Friends... And Their Best Friend!"

"Have You Prayed for a Child Lately?"

"CHILDREN NEED LOVE, ESPECIALLY WHEN THEY DON'T DESERVE IT."

Harold S. Hulbert

"A torn jacket is soon mended, but hard words bruise the heart of a child."

Henry Wadsworth Longfellow

"I think that saving a little child and bringing him into his own, is a derned sight better business than loafing around the throne."

John Hay

"GOD SENDS CHILDREN FOR ANOTHER PURPOSE THAN MERELY TO KEEP UP THE RACE — TO ENLARGE OUR HEARTS AND TO MAKE US UNSELFISH."

Mary Howitt

Quiz Show:
Puppet vs Staff

This skit requires five well-known and respected leaders of your congregation who can be good sports about being foils for a puppet. Insert the titles and names of these church staff members or other leaders. Also, adapt the information about the various children's ministries to fit those you offer.

M.C.: We are proud to present an exciting contest of Bible knowledge—featuring the members of our church staff—our Pastor, Youth Director, Music Director, Office Secretary and a Board Member—against a typical child from our children's ministries. That sounds about even. So, Staff, are you ready?

Staff: Yo! Right on! Let's do it!

M.C.: Sally, are you ready?

Sally: (puppet): I sure am!

M.C.: The first question is for our Pastor. After the battle of Jericho, where did Joshua bury the survivors?

Pastor: The Dead Sea? Get it? The DEAD Sea?

M.C.: Try again, Pastor.

Pastor: (Name of local cemetery)?

M.C.: Sorry, Pastor. Sally, do you know where Joshua buried the survivors of the battle of Jericho?

Sally: You don't bury survivors!

M.C.: Correct! One point for Sally—and our next question is for our Youth Director. Who was the shortest man in the Bible?

Youth Director: Zacchaeus? The little man who climbed the tree to see Jesus?

M.C.: Sorry. Sally, who was the smallest man in the Bible?

Sally: That's easy! Bildad the Shuhite. Get it? Shoe—height!

Staff: Groan!!

M.C.: Right again! You have two points, Sally. Let's see how our Music Director can do on this next question. How many animals did Moses take on the ark?

Music Director: According to Genesis 6 and 7 he took two of each species that was considered unclean and seven pairs of every clean species.

M.C.: Sorry. Sally?

Sally: MOSES didn't take any animals on the ark! NOAH did!

M.C.: You're on a roll, Sally. Let's see how our Office Secretary does with this next question. Where was Abraham when the lights went out?

Secretary: Egypt? Haran? Hebron? Mount Sinai?

M.C.: Good try. Sally, do you know where Abraham was when the lights went out?

Sally: In the dark!

M.C.: Boy, you're sharp today, Sally. Let's see if one of our Board Members can win this last point for the staff. Who were the first three men Jesus chose to be His epistles?

Board Member: Peter, James and John.

M.C.: I'm really sorry. Sally?

Sally: Jesus didn't choose ANY epistles. He chose APOSTLES!

M.C.: Wow, Sally, how did you get so smart?

Sally: Well, I never miss Sunday School every Sunday morning at _____.

M.C.: Are all the kids who come to Sunday School this smart?

Sally: Oh, no! I'm the smartest.

M.C.: I see.

Sally: I'm also the best singer in the children's choir that practices on

_____.

M.C.: I see.

Sally: And I'm the best ringer in the handbell choir that practices on _____.

M.C.: I see.

Sally: And I graduated with highest honors from the church preschool.

M.C.: I see.

Sally: And the teachers who take care of kids in the nursery and children's church during Sunday morning worship always say they like me best.

M.C.: I see.

Sally: And I win more awards than anyone at VBS every summer.

M.C.: I see. Anything else we should know about you?

Sally: Besides my naturally curly hair?

M.C.: Besides that.

Sally: And my captivating smile?

M.C.: Not counting that.

Sally: Well, I'm also very good at being humble.

M.C.: (To audience.) Not all of the kids who participate in our children's ministries are as exceptional as Sally, but they are all very special to God—and to us. If you're a parent, one of the best things you can do for your child is to bring him or her regularly to Sunday School every Sunday morning and to children's choir on _____. (To Sally.) Sally, is there anything you'd like to say to all these nice people about our children's ministries?

Sally: I thought you'd never ask. (To audience.) I'd just like to say, we need grown-ups like you to be our friends, to learn our names and say "Hi" when we run—I mean when we walk—past you.

M.C.: Good idea, Sally.

Sally: And we need some of you to be our special friends on Sunday morning in Sunday School or in our children's music programs.

M.C.: Thank you, Sally.

Sally: (Getting louder.) So before you leave, talk to _____ —she's the (lady who leads the children's choir) or look for _____ (he's the nicest man I know) and find out how you can be a special friend to a child this year!

M.C.: (To audience.) I guess she said it all. Thank you.

Sunday School Special

This skit is effective in introducing expressions of appreciation for those involved in the Sunday School, for thanking the congregation for supporting children's ministry, or encouraging people to invite and bring neighborhood children to Sunday School.

Jeremy: (Shouting.) Hey, Morgan! Come on out! I've got something to ask you!

Morgan: (Offstage.) Just a minute, Jeremy! I'm tying my shoes.

Jeremy: You'd better hurry, Morgan. This is important!

Morgan: (Offstage.) I'm coming! I'm coming! (Enters.) I'm here! So what's up?

Jeremy: I came over to ask if you can go to Sunday School with me tomorrow.

Morgan: Sunday School? I already go to school five days a week. Why would I want to go to school on Sunday?

Jeremy: Because it's a lot better than regular school. That's why we call it Sunday School. It's special!

Morgan: So, why don't they call it Special School?

Jeremy: Because no one would know what day to come.

Morgan: Makes sense, I guess. But what do you do at Special School, I mean Sunday School?

Jeremy: What do we do? We do lots of stuff! Neat stuff!

Morgan: What kind of neat stuff?

Jeremy: *A*, we have art projects, *B*, we have Bible stories, *C*, we have contests, *D*, we have drama, *E*, we have...

Morgan: I'll bet you don't have anything for *Q* or *X* or *Z*.

Jeremy: *Q*, we have quizzes, *X* we have excitement,...

Morgan: That's cheating!

Jeremy: It was close enough... and *Z*, we have,... we have,...

Morgan: I knew you couldn't do it!

Jeremy: And *Z*, we have a zillion other neat things!

Morgan: Wow! A zillion! When is this Sunday School?

Jeremy: On Sunday!

Morgan: I knew that! I want to know what TIME on Sunday!

Jeremy: It starts at 9:30! How about if we pick you up at 9:00 and we can be there a little early, 'cause our teachers always have some neat stuff ready, and we can get a head start on some of the other kids.

Morgan: You're sure I'm gonna like it?

Jeremy: Well, not totally sure. Remember, you're a little weird about things you like and don't like. (Exits.)

Morgan: (On the way out.) What do you mean I'm weird? You're the one who eats library paste and won't try chocolate-covered cucumbers! (Exits.)

Leader: I think both Jeremy and Morgan may have rather weird taste in snacks, but I'm sure that won't affect their enjoyment of our Sunday School. Every week a terrific team of teachers provide children with a marvelous hour of learning, packed with everything from *A* to *Z*—with possibly a few exceptions. On behalf of our children and their teachers, I want to express appreciation for the outstanding support you have given so that our children's ministry can continue to show God's love to the children of our church and our community.

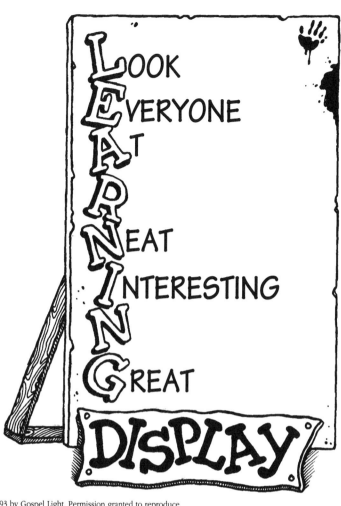

LOOK
EVERYONE
AT
GREAT
INTERESTING
GREAT

LEARNING

DISPLAY

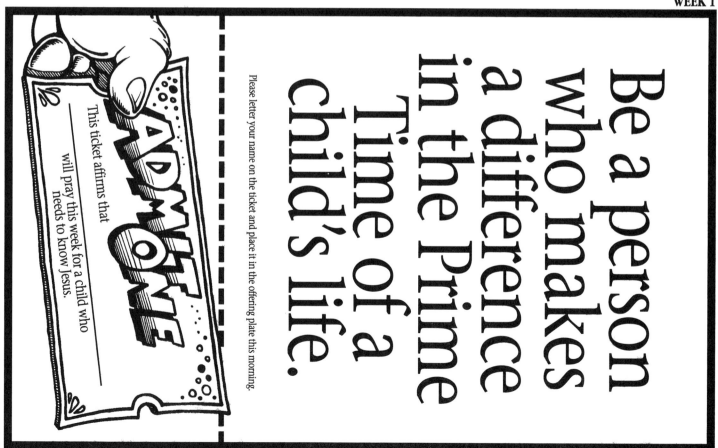

Be a person who makes a difference in the Prime Time of a child's life.

Please letter your name on the ticket and place it in the offering plate this morning.

This ticket affirms that

_____

will pray this week for a child who needs to know Jesus.

ADMIT ONE

THE CHILDHOOD YEARS ARE A PRIME TIME OF LIFE.

SUNDAY MORNING IS THE PRIME TIME OF THE WEEK.

Prime Time for Kids begins next Sunday morning. You can help parents and kids become part of the excitement!

Please letter your name on the ticket and place it in the offering plate this morning.

This ticket promises that _____ will pray for the parent of a child during the coming week.

ADMIT ONE

TELEVISION ABSORBS MORE THAN 20 HOURS OF THE AVERAGE CHILD'S WEEK.

SCHOOL INVOLVES A CHILD FOR MORE THAN 30 HOURS PER WEEK, PLUS ANOTHER 3 TO 7 HOURS OF HOMEWORK.

◆

LITTLE LEAGUE OFTEN REQUIRES 5 OR MORE HOURS PER WEEK.

◆

MUSIC LESSONS EXPECT 2 TO 4 HOURS PER WEEK.

◆

THE CHURCH AVERAGES LESS THAN 1 HOUR PER WEEK OF EFFECTIVE PERSONAL AND SPIRITUAL GUIDANCE.

Please letter your name on the ticket and place it in the offering plate this morning.

This ticket promises that _____ will invite a child to attend Prime Time for Kids.

Name of Child _____
Phone _____

ADMIT ONE

TO BE A CHILD IS TO KNOW THE FUN OF LIVING.
TO HAVE A CHILD IS TO KNOW THE BEAUTY OF LIFE.
TO TEACH A CHILD IS TO KNOW THE JOY OF GIVING.

A child needs you to be a special person in the Prime Time of life. And you need a child who will be close enough to you to help you sense the joy and delight of being God's child in this stress-filled world.

Please letter your name on the ticket and place it in the offering plate this morning.

This ticket authorizes the Children's Ministry Team to admit:

ADMIT ONE

Name _____

Phone _____

for consideration as a member of the team — as someone who cares about children and wants to be involved in sharing God's love with them.

Class: _____
Location: _____
Teacher: _____

A Teacher I Remember

SUNDAY SCHOOL MEMORIES

Please
Pray
For Our
Children

Class:

Teacher:

**PRAYER
REMINDER**

Prayer Partner
MEMO

MY PARTNER:

CLASS:

PRAY FOR:

I
WILL
PRAY
FOR

Contact the Community

A ministry to children which only touches the children of church families is a ministry doomed to a gradual but steady decline. For most of its more than 200 year history, the Sunday School has seen outreach as a major reason for its existence. However, during the past 30 years and for a wide variety of reasons, that objective has been lost in a large percentage of churches. Some of those reasons are reflected in these "typical" statements:

✦ "I can barely handle the children who attend now. Why would I want to try bringing in more children?" (Typical Teacher)

✦ "I can barely recruit enough teachers to handle the children we have now. How would I possibly get enough teachers if we started bringing in kids from outside?" (Typical Leader)

✦ "Bring some neighborhood kids to Sunday School with us? But then we'd be pretty much obligated to come every Sunday. And we like to go out for brunch after church. Speaking of church, would we have to sit with them during the worship service?" (Typical Church Member)

✦ "We spent a lot of money in building nice facilities. If we bring in a bunch of unchurched kids, they'll mark up the walls and spill things on the carpets." (Typical Board Member)

✦ "First Whatsits Church tripled their attendance in three years by using the Proselytizing Prodigals Program. We're switching all our outreach efforts there." (Typical Pastor)

✦ "It's simply not cost effective in today's economy to build more education space, especially if it's only used a few times a week. Besides, we recommend that churches focus their building program on big auditoriums or sanctuaries which can be used a few times a week." (Typical Consultant)

✦ "My professor told me to focus on reaching adults rather than children. I'm not quite sure how to do that, but it sounds good to me." (Typical Seminarian)

Now that we have offended (gently, we hope) just about everyone, we do feel compelled to point out that, whatever the reasons, however valid or not, when a Sunday School (or any other agency of the church) loses its emphasis on outreach, the inevitable result is a decline. This decline is reflected in many ways:

✦ Attendance levels off and then decreases.

✦ Teachers and other workers stop seeing new people coming in, and their motivation and commitment levels drop.

✦ The church (pastor, leaders, members, etc.) stops viewing Sunday School as a vital ministry.

A decline in one program would not be a major cause for concern if other programs effectively take up the slack. Unfortunately, few, if any, churches have successfully put something else in the place of the Sunday School. This experience is causing many church leaders who have neglected the Sunday School for several decades to start giving it the attention it deserves.

All of the above discussion would be of merely academic interest, however, if it were not for three significant truths:

1. Large numbers of children in your community will respond positively to attractive invitations to attend your Sunday School.

2. Large numbers of unchurched families will respond positively to attractive invitations for their children to attend your Sunday School.

3. Reaching a child with the love of Christ is one of the most effective ways to reach the parents. As one parent told a friend recently, "I think it's time for our family to start talking about coming to church together. Our child has really been discipling us."

Therefore, this chapter contains resources and ideas to build bridges to nonchurched families and their children.

Handouts/Invitations

PP.213-237 Reproducible

Every church needs an attractive, brief handout that introduces your children's ministries. This flier or brochure is a useful tool for both long-time residents and newcomers in the community, and should contain a friendly invitation for a child to attend.

Uses for a Handout

✦ Distribute it throughout the church neighborhood and in areas where church members live.

✦ Post it on supermarket windows or bulletin boards.

✦ Include it as part of the local Welcome Wagon kit.

✦ Encourage church parents and children to give them out to their friends.

✦ Encourage church members to set it out in their businesses.

✦ Mail them to new residents.

✦ Give them out in a new housing tract.

Guidelines for Writing the Handout

✦ Handout can be a full-page sheet, a folded half-page flier or even a postcard.

✦ Include attractive graphics (see pages 213-237 in this chapter and pages 87-91 in chapter 3) and plenty of white space.

✦ Briefly state the goals of your ministry, phrasing them to have meaning for people who are unfamiliar with church terminology. For example: "Our purpose is to help your child build lasting friendships, enjoy interesting activities, and discover the truth of God's love and goodness."

✦ In short, specific sentences, briefly describe how families and children will benefit. For example, "Each child will receive warm, personal attention from our staff of trained volunteers. Parents will enjoy the security of knowing their child is safe and receiving positive encouragement to develop sound personal values."

✦ Include essential facts (church name, location, phone number, and current ministries). Do not include information that changes frequently, unless you plan to redo the handout often. (Costs, dates, time, leaders' names, etc.)

✦ Periodically produce handouts which focus on a particular feature as a way to get people's attention. For example, use a seasonal emphasis to promote Christmas, Easter, or summer events. (See "Seasonal Ideas" section on pages 83-85 in chapter 3 for help with these ideas.) The start of the school year or the beginning of a new year is a good time for a focused handout. Plus, anytime you plan a special event for kids and their families, develop a handout to use in spreading the word through the community. (See "Theme Days" section on pages 19-23 in chapter 2 for special event ideas.)

Friendship Day

PP.239-245 Reproducible

Once every year, plan a time when each regular attender is encouraged to bring a friend to Sunday School. This can be done within a single class or department, but is usually most effective when promoted throughout the entire Sunday School.

Promotion

Start announcing this day a full month in advance.

✦ Encourage children to identify a specific friend to invite.

✦ Emphasize that the intent is to do something good for this friend, not to twist anyone's arm to do something they might not want to do.

✦ Contact parents, suggesting that they can assist in bringing the friend. For example, parents can talk to the parents of the friend, even offering to have the friend "sleep over" the night before.

✦ Put up posters, pennants, banners or balloons a week or two in advance, creating a festive atmosphere.

Special Features

Encourage teachers to provide special refreshments, get-acquainted activities, and name tags for all to wear. (Notice the "I Brought a Friend" name tags on page 245.) Include some special feature guaranteed to interest children:

✦ puppets;

✦ video;

✦ special music;

✦ live animal friend (great for younger children);

✦ "Celebrity" guest (Kids will be as impressed to meet a high school or college athlete from your church—especially if he or she comes in uniform—as they would if you brought in a professional "star." Well, almost as impressed.) who can talk briefly about Jesus as our best friend for all of life.

A Few Guidelines

Be prepared to handle extra children that Sunday. Things to consider include:

✦ Welcoming visitors—enlist friendly, outgoing people to serve as greeters at main entrances.

✦ Space, equipment, chairs and supplies—will the usual physical arrangements need to be modified to accommodate a larger group? A few options to consider:

1. Remove all chairs and do all work standing around tables and/or seated on the floor.

2. Temporarily remove any unnecessary furniture (piano, desk, lectern or pulpit, etc.).

3. Remove some or all tables, doing work on floor or on walls. Choose lesson activities that adapt easily to large groups. Consider modifying student worksheet activities from your curriculum. For example, if there is a puzzle on the worksheet, copy the puzzle onto a large sheet of paper, overhead transparency or chalkboard, so that children may complete the puzzle in a large group.

Follow-up

Send "We're glad you came" cards (see pages 25-31 in chapter 2) to all visitors. Also make phone calls, inviting each child to a special event which has been planned to occur in the next week or so. See "Outreach Events" section in this chapter for event ideas.

Newspaper/ Radio

Local newspaper and radio announcements can be effective ways of alerting the community about your children's programs. Options include paid advertising, free public service announcements, and straight news reporting. There are major benefits which can make it worthwhile to incur the expense and time of media promotion:

✦ Wide coverage—you can get your message quickly to a large audience in your community.

✦ Positive image—a good-quality media presentation gains credibility by association with the media outlet. For example, when people hear your radio spot, they are already predisposed to a positive reaction because they are usually listening to a station they like. In a society where many people are suspicious of religion and churches, association with a media outlet can improve people's responses.

✦ When done in conjunction with other efforts (distribution of handouts, personal invitations, etc.), media announcements increase the impact of the message.

Guidelines

1. Survey the kinds of ads, announcements and news stories that are currently being presented by your local papers and stations. Do they have regular features dealing with children and families? Are there specific reporters or announcers who tend to cover children and family issues? Are there particular times of day or sections of the newspaper which are targeted toward children or parents? Do not assume that the religion section of the newspaper or the church announcements on a Christian station are the best place for your message. If you are trying to reach non-Christians, your message may be more effective elsewhere.

2. Find out the deadlines, policies, costs and the format requirements of the outlet(s) you desire to use. A few phone calls can usually get the information you need.

3. When you actually submit material to be presented, be sure to include all the essential facts (who, what, when, where, why and how). Provide a name and phone number the station or newspaper can contact for further information.

4. Inform the station and/or newspaper of:

✦ special events (sports camp, VBS, parenting classes, etc.);

✦ an award or honor to someone associated with your Sunday School;

✦ an outreach or service project of community interest done by a class or the Sunday School;

✦ a unique aspect of your Sunday School, such as a special Sunday School class (e.g. class for blind or deaf children).

5. For newspaper ads, you may use the art and headlines on pages 213-217,235-237 in this chapter.

Special Interest Classes/ Workshops

Offer a short (one-week, a Saturday morning, Sunday or weekday evening, an afternoon after school, etc.) classes or workshops on topics of interest to either children or parents:

◆ craft or art classes;

◆ music classes;

◆ book clubs;

◆ family exercise/recreation (aerobics, volleyball, cycling, jogging, etc.);

◆ cooking classes;

◆ sports camps (soccer, basketball, volleyball, etc.);

◆ parenting classes (Preparing for Kindergarten, Bicycle Safety, Discipline, Getting Ready for Adolescence, Drug Proof Your Kids, etc.).

Guidelines for Organizing and Promoting

1. Identify people in your church who have interests and abilities in areas in which classes can be offered. Also consider people outside your church family who can be brought in for additional leadership help. For example, some churches use coaching staffs from nearby Christian colleges or schools to lead sports camps or recreation events. Or, contact a doctor, marriage and family counselor or other professional to lead or participate in a class on a particular topic.

2. Enlist a core of church families who will commit to participating in the event before public announcements are made. In some cases it may be necessary to limit the number of participants from the church in order to ensure that there is room for unchurched people you are trying to reach. One way to do this is to require that a church family can participate only if they sign up someone from outside the church. Emphasize to church families that the intent is to reach people who do not attend any church, not to fill up the event with people from other churches.

Connecting the Class to Church Ministries

1. Ask a representative of the church (a pastor or lay leader) to be present and to welcome participants to the event. Include a brief statement on why the church is sponsoring this activity: "We are deeply committed to helping families in our communities by providing a well-rounded diet of wholesome activities."

2. Have available at the event copies of your handout about Sunday School and/or other children's ministries. In some cases, you may just want to have them available for people to pick up. In other cases, you may want to distribute them to everyone (e.g., attach them to a registration card).

3. Put up an attractive poster or two announcing other children's events.

4. Take similar advantage of any other classes or groups (e.g., a preschool) which meet in your buildings.

Follow Up on Families

Send "We're glad you came" cards (see pages 25-31 in chapter 2) to all participants. Also make a phone call inviting the family to a special event which has been planned to occur in the next week or so. (See "Outreach Events" section in this chapter for ideas.)

Outreach Events

Periodically plan special events to which children can invite friends, or to which church families can invite other families. Specifically plan such an event or events soon after special programs when visitors are expected (Friendship Day, VBS, Easter Sunday, special class/workshop, etc.).

In addition to events planned for all children, encourage individual classes and departments to occasionally organize an event for their age-group. (See "Class Parties" section on page 18 in chapter 2.)

Decide whether the event will be one you plan and conduct, or whether you go as a group to something being offered in your area:

◆ hiking or cycling (For older children, have a teacher or parent go ahead of the group, marking the route the group has to follow. At the end of the route serve refreshments and play several games.);

◆ snow sledding, roller or ice skating, swimming or surfing;

◆ amusement park, fair or zoo;

◆ tour a place of interest: historic monument, planetarium, TV studio, factory, museum;

◆ pizza picnic in the park;

- family movie/video series;

- music concert or puppet show;

- high school, college or professional athletic event;

- fun athletic competition—crazy games, miniature golf, swimming, kite-flying contests, family bowling tournament, etc.;

- novelty parties—scavenger hunt, progressive dinners, pet parade, build your own ice cream sundae, etc.

Guidelines

1. Focus promotional efforts on children or parents who have been recent visitors to the class.

2. Enlist enough adult help to provide safe supervision for all children. A parental permission form should be completed for each child. All drivers should have adequate insurance coverage and seat belts for all passengers.

3. Involve parents as much as possible (transportation, refreshments, games, etc.), seeking to link up those who attend regularly with those who are new or "on the fringe."

4. Plan times when leaders and teachers can build relationships with new children and parents. Avoid having the staff work so hard to keep the event going that they are unable to sit down and chat. Look for opportunities to invite guests to Sunday School or other children's ministries.

5. Enlist people to pray daily for the event and for the people who will be invited to attend.

Follow-up

1. A few days after an outreach event, send a card or letter inviting the child and/or parent to Sunday School or other children's ministry.

2. Also send a card or letter to those children or families who brought a guest. Encourage them to continue building friendships, to pray regularly for their friends, and to personally invite their friends again. Emphasize that if their friends had a good time at a recent event, right now may be the best time ever to encourage that friend to start attending regularly.

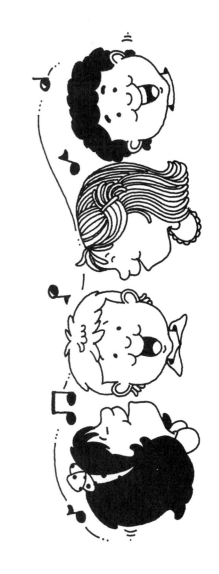

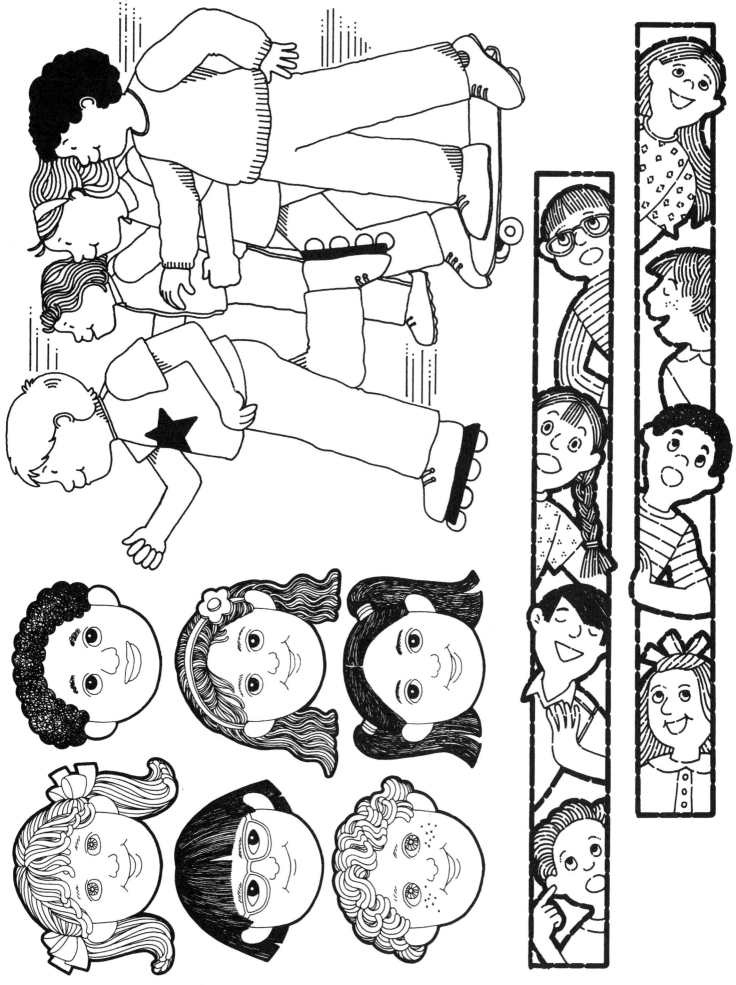

ADMIT ONE

Date:

Time:

Place:

For:

Take Note!

Who:

What:

When:

Where:

SUPER!

IT'S TIME!

SIGN UP NOW!

Don't Miss Out!

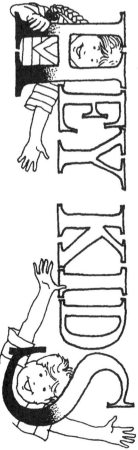

HEY KIDS

It's A
Family Affair!

A GREAT PLACE FOR KIDS

Follow The Crowd...

Check It Out!

PARENTS

FAMILY ACTIVITIES

Listen Up!

GET READY

What's Happening?

SPECIAL PROGRAMS

COME ON OVER!

You're INVITED

Join Us!

FOCUS ON FAMILIES

SIGN UP!

LOOK What's New

Children's ♪ Music

Children's ♪ Choir

Children's Ministries

Children's Programs

GET READY

KID NEWS

SUNDAY SCHOOL

Vacation Bible School

CHURCH SCHOOL

After School Programs
Midweek Programs
Summer Programs

Date:

Time:

Friendship Day

FRIENDSHIP DAY
✦ CHAPTER EIGHT ✦ 239

Bring a Friend!

FRIENDSHIP DAY

 # BRING A FRIEND!

 Friendship DAY

I BROUGHT
A FRIEND!

_____

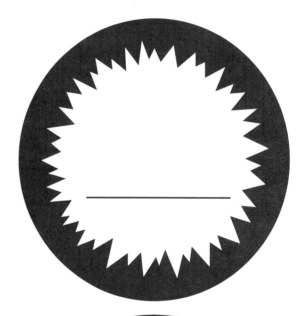

_____

I BROUGHT
A FRIEND!

_____

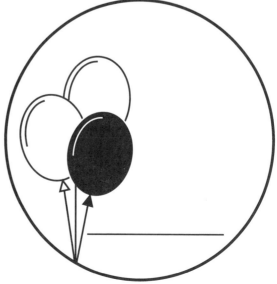

_____

Teacher Training Resources

Audiotapes

15-Minute Teacher Training

Today's life in the fast lane makes it almost impossible to schedule teacher training. These concentrated training tapes sum up the essentials of effective teaching in 15-minute bites, making them perfect for teachers on the move. Topics included are discipline, how to talk to children about salvation, understanding children and how to converse with children. Each set comes with two minute audiotapes and is reproducible for you to provide a set each of your teachers.

Series 1- Young Children, Ages 2-5;

Series 2- Children, Grades 1-6

Videotapes

How to Teach Young Children About God

Here's a video training session for teachers *and* parents! *How to Teach Young Children About God* shows how to relate God's love in ways young children can understand. Teachers and parents will discover that they have an important role as partners in Christian education.

Hugs and Fishes

Put a curious, active boy alone in a room next to a goldfish bowl and what do you think will happen? *Hugs and Fishes* shows that even the wildest antics of children are really opportunities for sharing God's love. And amazing things do happen when ordinary people make a faith commitment to teach Sunday School. This video will inspire the members of your church to take a fresh look at Sunday School as a vital tool for developing the Christian leaders of the future.

Clip Art Books

The Big Picture Bible Time Line Book

These reproducible pages make a 60-foot (18-m) time line showing the sequence of events in the Bible. Use for coloring activities or place around the room to help children track their progress through Scripture.

The Complete Bible Story Clip Art Book

Makes your lessons, fliers and handouts come alive. Includes pictures of Bible events, characters and places.

The Kids' Worker's Clip Art Book

Over 1,000 reproducible illustrations for teachers and others who love to work with kids.

The One Minute Poster Book

A dream come true for anyone who needs to publicize an event at church. It contains premade posters and fliers for every church event imaginable.

The Sunday School Clip Art Book

Produce great looking mailers, fliers, letters, invitations, brochures and announcements for your Sunday School. Follow the step-by-step instructions.

Teacher Training Resources

Books

Everything You Want to Know About Teaching Young Children, Birth-6 Years

Wes Haystead

This handbook is designed to enable adults at church, home and school to better understand how young children learn and grow and how to meet their God-created needs.

Everything You Want to Know About Teaching Children, Grades 1-6

Barbara Bolton, Charles T. Smith and Wes Haystead

This handbook is designed to give the new as well as the experienced teacher fresh insights and practical plans for effectively teaching God's Word.

Sunday School Smart Pages

edited by Wes and Sheryl Haystead

Every children's worker occasionally runs into a question and doesn't know where to turn. Now you can let your fingers do the footwork to come up with advice, answers and articles on every aspect of teaching children. This book is a comprehensive library of resources for children's workers. It also contains reproducible clip art for fliers, handouts and classroom posters, as well as reproducible articles and worksheets.